Tom Tiddler's Ground: A Christmas Budget

Charles Dickens

Price Twenty-five Cents.

TOM TIDDLER'S GROUND.

A Christmas Budget.

By Charles Dickens

AND OTHERS.

NEW YORK:

Carleton, Publisher, 130 Grand St.

(LATE RUDD & CARLETON.)

M DCCC LXI.

Author of "Pickwick Papers," "Nicholas Nickleby," "Dombey and Son,"

"Great Expectations," "David Copperfield," "Barnaby Rudge," etc.

A Christmas Story for 1861.

TOM TIDDLER'S GROUND.

𝔄 𝔆𝔥𝔯𝔦𝔰𝔱𝔪𝔞𝔰 𝔅𝔲𝔡𝔤𝔢𝔱.

BY CHARLES DICKENS

AND OTHERS.

NEW YORK:

CARLETON, PUBLISHER, 130 GRAND STREET.

(LATE RUDD & CARLETON.)

M DCCC LXI.

Feb 13, 1941

Goodspeed's Book Shop

Printed from the Author's Advance Sheets.

———•———

CONTENTS.

H

TOM TIDDLER'S GROUND.

I.

PICKING UP SOOT AND CINDERS.

"AND why Tom Tiddler's ground?" asked the Traveller.

"Because he scatters halfpence to Tramps and such-like," returned the Landlord, "and of course they pick 'em up. And this being done on his own land (which it *is* his own land, you observe, and were his family's before him), why it is but regarding the halfpence as gold and silver, and turning the ownership of the property a bit round your finger, and there you have the name of the children's game complete. And it's appropriate too," said the Landlord, with his favourite action of stooping a little, to look across the table out of window. at vacancy, under the window-blind which was half drawn down. "Leastwise it has been so considered by many gentlemen which have partook of chops and tea in the present humble parlour."

The traveller was partaking of chops and tea in the present humble parlour, and the Landlord's shot was fired obliquely at him.

"And you call him a Hermit?" said the Traveller.

"They call him such," returned the Landlord, evading personal responsibility; "he is in general so considered."

"What *is* a Hermit?" asked the Traveller.

"What is it?" repeated the Landlord, drawing his hand across his chin.

"Yes, what is it?"

The Landlord stooped again, to get a more comprehensive view of vacancy under the window-blind, and—with an asphyxiated appearance on him as one unaccustomed to definition—made no answer.

"I'll tell you what I suppose it to be," said the Traveller. "An abominably dirty thing."

"Mr. Mopes is dirty, it cannot be denied," said the Landlord.

"Intolerably conceited."

"Mr. Mopes is vain of the life he leads, some do say," replied the Landlord, as another concession.

"A slothful unsavoury nasty reversal of the laws of human nature," said the Traveller; "and for the sake of GOD's working world and its wholesomeness, both moral and physical, I would put the thing on the treadmill (if I had my way) wherever I found it; whether on a pillar, or in a hole; whether on Tom Tiddler's ground, or the Pope of Rome's ground, or a Hindoo fakeer's ground, or any other ground."

"I don't know about putting Mr. Mopes on the treadmill," said the Landlord, shaking his head very seriously. "There ain't a doubt but what he has got landed property."

"How far may it be to this said Tom Tiddler's ground?" asked the Traveller.

"Put it at five mile," returned the Landlord.

"Well! When I have done my breakfast," said the Traveller, "I'll go there. I came over here this morning, to find it out and see it."

"Many does," observed the Landlord.

The conversation passed, in the Midsummer weather of no remote year of grace, down among the pleasant dales and trout-streams of a green English county. No matter what county. Enough that you may hunt there, shoot there, fish there, traverse long grass-grown Roman roads there, open ancient barrows there, see many a square mile of richly cultivated land there, and hold Arcadian talk with a bold peasantry, their country's pride, who will tell you (if you want to know) how pastoral housekeeping is done on nine shillings a week.

Mr. Traveller sat at his breakfast in the little sanded parlour of the Peal of Bells village alehouse, with the dew and dust of an early walk upon his shoes—an early walk by road and meadow and coppice, that had sprinkled him bountifully with little blades of grass, and scraps of new hay, and with leaves both young and old, and with other such fragrant tokens of the freshness and wealth of summer. The window through which the landlord had concentrated his gaze upon vacancy, was shaded, because the morning sun was hot and bright on the village street. The village street was like most other village streets: wide for its height, silent for its size, and drowsy in the dullest degree. The quietest little dwellings with the largest of window-shutters (to shut up Nothing as carefully as if it were the Mint, or the

Bank of England) had called in the Doctor's house so suddenly, that his brass door-plate and three stories stood among them as conspicuous and different as the Doctor himself in his broadcloth, among the smock-frocks of his patients. The village residences seemed to have gone to law with a similar absence of consideration, for a score of weak little lath-and-plaster cabins clung in confusion about the Attorney's red-brick house, which, with glaring door-steps and a most terrific scraper, seemed to serve all manner of ejectments upon them. They were as various as labourers—high-shouldered, wry-necked, one-eyed, goggle-eyed, squinting, bow-legged, knock-knee'd, rheumatic, crazy. Some of the small tradesmen's houses, such as the crockery-shop and the harness-maker's, had a Cyclops window in the middle of the gable, within an inch or two of its apex, suggesting that some forlorn rural Prentice must wriggle himself into that apartment horizontally, when he retired to rest, after the manner of the worm. So bountiful in its abundance was the surrounding country, and so lean and scant the village, that one might have thought the village had sown and planted everything it once possessed, to convert the same into crops. This would account for the bareness of the little shops, the bareness of the few boards and trestles designed for market purposes in a corner of the street, the bareness of the obsolete Inn and Inn Yard, with the ominous inscription " Excise Office," not yet faded out from the gateway, as indicating the very last thing that poverty could get rid of. This would also account for the determined abandonment of the village by one stray dog, fast lessening in the perspective where the white posts and the pond were, and would explain his conduct on the hypothesis that he was going (through the act of suicide) to convert himself into manure, and become a part proprietor in turnips or mangold-wurzel.

Mr. Traveller having finished his breakfast and paid his moderate score, walked out to the threshold of the Peal of Bells, and, thence directed by the pointing finger of his host, betook himself towards the ruined hermitage of Mr. Mopes the hermit.

For, Mr. Mopes, by suffering everything about him to go to ruin, and by dressing himself in a blanket and skewer, and by steeping himself in soot and grease and other nastiness, had acquired great renown in all that country-side—far greater renown than he could ever have won for himself, if his career had been that of any ordinary Christian, or decent Hottentot. He had even blanketed and skewered and sooted and greased himself into the London papers. And it was curious to find, as Mr. Traveller found by stopping for a new direction at this farm-house or at that cottage as he went along, with how much accuracy the morbid Mopes had counted on the weakness of his neighbours to embellish him. A mist of home-brewed marvel and romance surrounded Mopes, in which (as in all fogs) the real proportions of the real object were extravagantly heightened. He had murdered his beautiful beloved in a fit of jealousy and was doing penance; he had made a vow under the influence of grief; he had made a vow under the influence of a fatal accident; he had made a vow under the influence of religion;

he had made a vow under the influence of drink; he had made a vow under the influence of disappointment; he had never made any vow, but " had got led into it" by the possession of a mighty and most awful secret; he was enormously rich, he was stupendously charitable, he was profoundly learned, he saw spectres, he knew and could do all kinds of wonders. Some said he went out every night, and was met by terrified wayfarers stalking along dark roads, others said he never went;out, some knew his penance to be nearly expired, others had positive information that his seclusion was not a penance at all, and would never expire but with himself. Even, as to the easy facts of how old he was, or how long he had held verminous occupation of his blanket and skewer, no consistent information was to be got, from those who must know if they would. He was represented as being all the ages between five-and-twenty and sixty, and as having been a hermit seven years, twelve, twenty, thirty—though twenty, on the whole, appeared the favourite term.

" Well, well!" said Mr. Traveller. "At any rate, let us see what a real live Hermit looks like."

So, Mr. Traveller went on, and on, and on, until he came to Tom Tiddler's Ground.

It was a nook in a rustic by-road, which the genius of Mopes had laid waste as completely, as if he had been born an Emperor and a Conqueror. Its centre object was a dwelling-house, sufficiently substantial, all the window-glass of which had been long ago abolished by the surprising genius of Mopes, and all the windows of which were barred across with rough-split logs of trees nailed over them on the outside. A rickyard, hip-high in vegetable rankness and ruin, contained outbuildings, from which the thatch had lightly fluttered away, on all the winds of all the seasons of the year, and from which the planks and beams had heavily dropped and rotted. The frosts and damps of winter, and the heats of summer, had warped what wreck remained, so that not a post or a board retained the position it was meant to hold, but everything was twisted from its purpose, like its owner, and degraded and debased. In this homestead of the sluggard, behind the ruined hedge, and sinking away among the ruined grass and the nettles, were the last perishing fragments of certain ricks: which had gradually mildewed and collapsed, until they looked like mounds of rotten honey-comb, or dirty sponge. Tom Tiddler's ground could even show its ruined water ; for, there was a slimy pond into which a tree or two had fallen—one soppy trunk and branches lay across it then—which in its accumulation of stagnant weed, and in its black decomposition, and in all its foulness and filth, was almost comforting, regarded as the only water that could have reflected the shameful place without seeming polluted by that low office.

Mr. Traveller looked all around him on Tom Tiddler's ground, and his glance at last encountered a dusty Tinker lying among the weeds and rank grass, in the shade of the dwelling-house. A rough walking-staff lay on the ground by his side, and his head rested on a small wallet. He met Mr. Traveller's eye without lifting up his head, merely depressing his chin a little (for he was lying on his back) to get a better view of him.

"Good day!" said Mr. Traveller.

"Same to you, if you like it," returned the Tinker.

"Don't *you* like it? It's a very fine day."

"I ain't partickler in weather," returned the Tinker, with a yawn.

Mr. Traveller had walked up to where he lay, and was looking down at him. "This is a curious place," said Mr. Traveller.

"Ay, I suppose so!" returned the Tinker. "Tom Tiddler's ground, they call this."

"Are you well acquainted with it?"

"Never saw it afore to-day," said the Tinker, with another yawn, "and don't care if I never see it again. There was a man here just now, told me what it was called. If you want to see Tom himself, you must go in at that gate." He faintly indicated with his chin, a little mean ruin of a wooden gate at the side of the house.

"Have you seen Tom?"

"No, and I ain't partickler to see him. I can see a dirty man anywhere."

"He does not live in the house, then?" said Mr. Traveller, casting his eyes upon the house anew.

"The man said," returned the Tinker, rather irritably,—"him as was here just now,—'this what you're a lying on, mate, is Tom Tiddler's ground. And if you want to see Tom,' he says, 'you must go in at that gate.' The man come out at that gate himself, and he ought to know."

"Certainly," said Mr. Traveller.

"Though, perhaps," exclaimed the Tinker, so struck by the brightness of his own idea, that it had the electric effect upon him of causing him to lift up his head an inch or so, "perhaps he was a liar! He told some rum'uns—him as was here just now, did—about this place of Tom's. He says—him as was here just now—'When Tom shut up the house, mate, to go to rack, the beds was left, all made, like as if somebody was a going to sleep in every bed. And if you was to walk through the bedrooms now, you'd see the ragged mouldy bedclothes a heaving and a heaving like seas. And a heaving and a heaving with what?' he says. 'Why, with the rats under 'em'"

"I wish I had seen that man," Mr. Traveller remarked.

"You'd have been welcome to see him instead of me seeing him," growled the Tinker; "for he was a long-winded one."

Not without a sense of injury in the remembrance, the Tinker gloomily closed his eyes. Mr. Traveller, deeming the Tinker a short-winded one, from whom no further breath of information was to be derived, betook himself to the gate.

Swung upon its rusty hinges, it admitted him into a yard in which there was nothing to be seen but an outhouse attached to the ruined building, with a barred window in it. As there were traces of many recent footsteps under this window, and as it was a low window, and unglazed, Mr. Traveller made bold to peep within the bars. And there to be sure he had a real live Hermit before him, and could judge how the real dead Hermits used to look.

He was lying on a bank of soot and cinders, on the floor, in front of a rusty fireplace. There was nothing else in the dark little kitchen, or scullery, or whatever his den had been originally used as, but a table with a litter of old bottles on it. A rat made a clatter among these bottles, jumped down, and ran over the real live Hermit on his way to his hole, or the man in *his* hole would not have been so easily discernible. Tickled in the face by the rat's tail, the owner of Tom Tiddler's ground opened his eyes, saw Mr. Traveller, started up, and sprang to the window.

"Humph!" thought Mr. Traveller, retiring a pace or two from the bars. "A compound of Newgate, Bedlam, a Debtors' Prison in the worst time, a chimney-sweep, a mudlark, and the Noble Savage! A nice old family, the Hermit family. Hah!"

Mr. Traveller thought this, as he silently confronted the sooty object in the blanket and skewer (in sober truth it wore nothing else), with the matted hair and the staring eyes. Further, Mr. Traveller thought, as the eyes surveyed him with a very obvious curiosity in ascertaining the effect they produced, "Vanity, vanity, vanity! Verily, all is vanity!"

"What is your name, sir, and where do you come from?" asked Mr. Mopes the Hermit—with an air of authority, but in the ordinary human speech of one who has been to school.

Mr. Traveller answered the inquiries.

"Did you come here, sir, to see *me*?"

"I did. I heard of you, and I came to see you. —I know you like to be seen." Mr. Traveller coolly threw the last words in, as a matter of course, to forestal an affectation of resentment or objection that he saw rising beneath the grease and grime of the face. They had their effect.

"So," said the Hermit, after a momentary silence, unclasping the bars by which he had previously held, and seating himself behind them on the ledge of the window, with his bare legs and feet crouched up, "you know I like to be seen?"

Mr. Traveller looked about him for something to sit on, and, observing a billet of wood in a corner, brought it near the window. Deliberately seating himself upon it, he answered: "Just so."

Each looked at the other, and each appeared to take some pains to get the measure of the other.

"Then you have come to ask me why I lead this life," said the Hermit, frowning in a stormy manner. "I never tell that to any human being. I will not be asked that."

"Certainly you will not be asked that by me," said Mr. Traveller, "for I have not the slightest desire to know."

"You are an uncouth man," said Mr. Mopes the Hermit.

"You are another," said Mr Traveller.

The Hermit, who was plainly in the habit of overawing his visitors with the novelty of his filth and his blanket and skewer, glared at his present visitor in some discomfiture and surprise: as if he had taken aim at him with a sure gun, and his piece had missed fire.

"Why do you come here at all?" he asked, after a pause.

"Upon my life," said Mr. Traveller, "I was made to ask myself that very question only a few minutes ago—by a Tinker too."

As he glanced towards the gate in saying it, the hermit glanced in that direction likewise.

"Yes. He is lying on his back in the sunlight outside," said Mr. Traveller, as if he had been asked concerning the man, "and he won't come in; for he says—and really very reasonably—'What should I come in for? I can see a dirty man anywhere.'"

"You are an insolent person. Go away from my premises. Go!" said the Hermit, in an imperious and angry tone.

"Come, come!" returned Mr. Traveller, quite undisturbed. "This is a little too much. You are not going to call yourself clean? Look at your legs. And as to these being your premises: —they are in far too disgraceful a condition to claim any privilege of ownership, or anything else."

The Hermit bounced down from his window-ledge, and cast himself on his bed of soot and cinders.

"I am not going," said Mr. Traveller, glancing in after him: "you won't get rid of me in that way. You had better come and talk."

"I won't talk," said the Hermit, flouncing round to get his back towards the window.

"Then I will," said Mr. Traveller. "Why should you take it ill that I have no curiosity to know how you live this highly absurd and highly indecent life? When I contemplate a man in a state of disease, surely there is no moral obligation on me to be anxious to know how he took it."

After a short silence, the Hermit bounced up again, and came back to the barred window.

"What? You are not gone?" he said, affecting to have supposed that he was.

"Nor going," Mr. Traveller replied: "I design to pass this summer day here."

"How dare you come, sir, upon my premises——" the Hermit was returning, when his visitor interrupted him.

"Really, you know, you must not talk about your premises. I cannot allow such a place as this to be dignified with the name of premises."

"How dare you," said the Hermit, shaking his bars, "come in at my gate, to taunt me with being in a diseased state?"

"Why, Lord bless my soul," returned the other, very composedly, "you have not the face to say that you are in a wholesome state? Do allow me again to call your attention to your legs. Scrape yourself anywhere—with anything—and then tell me you are in a wholesome state. The fact is, Mr. Mopes, that you are not only a Nuisance——"

"A Nuisance?" repeated the Hermit, fiercely.

"What is a place in this obscene state of dilapidation but a Nuisance? What is a man in your obscene state of dilapidation but a Nuisance? Then, as you very well know, you cannot do without an audience, and your audience is a Nuisance. You attract all the disreputable vagabonds and prowlers within ten miles round, by exhibiting yourself to them in that objectionable blanket, and by throwing copper money among them, and

giving them drink out of those very dirty jars and bottles that I see in there (their stomachs need be strong!); and in short," said Mr. Traveller, summing up in a quietly and comfortably settled manner, "you are a Nuisance, and this kennel is a Nuisance, and the audience that you cannot possibly dispense with is a Nuisance, and the Nuisance is not merely a local Nuisance, because it is a general Nuisance to know that there can be such a Nuisance left in civilisation so very long after its time."

"Will you go away? I have a gun in here," said the Hermit.

"Pooh!"

"I have!"

"Now, I put it to you. Did I say you had not? And as to going away, didn't I say I am not going away? You made me forget where I was. I now remember that I was remarking on your conduct being a Nuisance. Moreover, it is in the last and, lowest degree inconsequent foolishness and weakness."

"Weakness?" echoed the Hermit.

"Weakness," said Mr. Traveller, with his former comfortably settled final air.

"I weak, you fool?" cried the Hermit, "I, who have held to my purpose, and my diet, and my only bed there, all these years?"

"The more the years, the weaker you," returned Mr. Traveller. "Though the years are not so many as folks say, and as you willingly take credit for. The crust upon your face is thick and dark, Mr. Mopes, but I can see enough of you through it, to see that you are still a young man."

"Inconsequent foolishness is lunacy, I suppose?" said the Hermit.

"I suppose it is very like it," answered Mr. Traveller.

"Do I converse like a lunatic?"

"One of us two must have a strong presumption against him of being one, whether or no. Either the clean and decorously clad man, or the dirty and indecorously clad man. I don't say which."

"Why, you self-sufficient bear," said the Hermit, "not a day passes but I am justified in my purpose by the conversations I hold here; not a day passes but I am shown, by everything I hear and see here, how right and strong I am in holding my purpose."

Mr. Traveller, lounging easily on his billet or wood, took out a pocket pipe and began to fill it. "Now, that a man," he said, appealing to the summer sky as he did so, "that a man—even behind bars, in a blanket and skewer—should tell me that he can see, from day to day, any orders or conditions of men, women, or children, who can by any possibility teach him that it is anything but the miserablest drivelling for a human creature to quarrel with his social nature—not to go so far as to say, to renounce his common human decency, for that is an extreme case; or who can teach him that he can in any wise separate himself from his kind and the habits of his kind, without becoming a deteriorated spectacle calculated to give the Devil (and perhaps the monkeys) pleasure; is something wonderful! I repeat," said Mr. Traveller, beginning to smoke, "the unreasoning hardihood of it, is is something wonderful—even in a man with the

dirt upon him an inch or two thick—behind bars
—in a blanket and skewer!"

The Hermit looked at him irresolutely, and retired to his soot and cinders and lay down, and
got up again, and came to the bars, and again
looked at him irresolutely, and finally said with
sharpness:

"I don't like tobacco."

"I don't like dirt," rejoined Mr. Traveller;
"tobacco is an excellent disinfectant. We shall
both be the better for my pipe. It is my inten-
tion to sit here through this summer day, until
that blessed summer sun sinks low in the west,
and to show you what a poor creature you are,
through the lips of every chance wayfarer who
may come in at your gate."

"What do you mean?" inquired the Hermit,
with a furious air.

"I mean that yonder is your gate, and there are
you, and here am I; I mean that I know it to be
a moral impossibility that any person can stray in
at that gate from any point of the compass, with
any sort of experience, gained at first hand, or
derived from another, that can confute me and
justify you."

"You are an arrogant and boastful hero," said
the Hermit. "You think yourself profoundly
wise."

"Bah!" returned Mr. Traveller, quietly smoking. "There is little wisdom in knowing that
every man must be up and doing, and that all
mankind are made dependent on one another."

"You have companions outside," said the Hermit. "I am not to be imposed upon by your
assumed confidence in the people who may enter."

"A depraved distrust," returned the visitor,
compassionately raising his eyebrows, "of course
belongs to your state. I can't help that."

"Do you mean to tell me you have no confede-
rates?"

"I mean to tell you nothing but what I have
told you. What I have told you, is, that it is a
moral impossibility that any son or daughter of
Adam can stand on this ground that I put my
foot on, or on any ground that mortal treads, and
gainsay the healthy tenure on which we hold our
existence."

"Which is," sneered the Hermit, "according to
you——"

"Which is," returned the other, "according to
Eternal Providence, that we must arise and wash
our faces and do our gregarious work, and act and
re-act on one another, leaving only the idiot and
the palsied to sit blinking in the corner. Come!"
apostrophising the gate; "Open Sesame! Show
his eyes and grieve his heart! I don't care who
comes, for I know what must come of it!"

With that, he faced round a little on his billet
of wood towards the gate; and Mr. Mopes the
Hermit, after two or three ridiculous bounces of
indecision at his bed and back again, submitted to
what he could not help himself against, and coiled
himself on his window-ledge, holding to his bars,
and looking out rather anxiously.

II.

PICKING UP EVENING SHADOWS.

THE first person to appear at the gate, was a
gentleman who looked in accidentally, and who
carried a sketch-book under his arm. From the
amazement and alarm expressed in his look and
manner, it was plain that the Hermit's fame had
not reached him. As soon as he could speak, he
mentioned apologetically that he had been struck,
as a stranger in that part of the country, by the
picturesquely-ruinous appearance of the yard and
out-houses, and that he had looked in at the gate,
with the idea of finding nothing more remarkable
than the materials for a sketch of still-life.

After revealing the mystery of the Hermit to
this bewildered stranger, Mr. Traveller explained
that any narrative-contributions towards the en-
livening of Mr. Mopes and the morning, drawn
from the personal experience of visitors at the
gate, would be highly appreciated in that mouldy
locality. At first, the visitor thus addressed hesi-
tated; not so much, as it afterwards appeared,
from want of means to answer the call made upon
him, as from want of resources in his own memory to use on the spur of the moment. Ponder-
ing on Mr. Traveller's request, he entered rather
absently into conversation with the Hermit.

"I never knew any good to come yet," said this
gentleman, "of a man shutting himself up in the
way you're doing. I know the temptation to it
myself, have experienced it myself, and yielded to
it myself; but I never knew any good—stop,
though," he added, correcting himself, as a scru-
pulous man does, who will not accept the help of
the smallest false statement to aid his dearest theory—"I do remember one good thing which came
in some degree, of a man's leading a solitary life."

The Hermit hugged his bars in triumph. Mr.
Traveller, nothing discouraged, requested the
stranger to mention the circumstance.

"You shall hear it," was the answer. "But,
before I begin, I must tell you that the period of
my tale dates some years back into the past, that
at the time of which I shall speak I had newly experienced a considerable reverse of fortune, and
that, fancying my friends would make me feel the
loss if I remained among them, I had determined
to shut myself up away from them, and lead an
entirely solitary life till I could in some degree
retrieve my losses."

IT is a tale, this that I am about to tell, of good
deeds revealed, of good instincts roused, of a good
work done, and a good result attained, and all
through Evening Shadows.

I have often thought what tell-tale things shadows are. I mean the shadows that one who
stands outside sees in the windows of a lighted-up
room or building; the shadows thrown on a blind
by figures interposing between it and the lamp-
light. I have noticed these in churches during
divine service, when I, wandering about outside,
have looked up at the windows and seen the
shades of a pair of lovers reading out of the same
hymn-book; of children evidently chattering and
grinning together; and sometimes a shadow

which bobbing forward from time to time, in a jerking fashion, then catching itself, still with a jerk, then remaining preternaturally erect and still, and then beginning to bob again, has suggested to me that the fourth head of a sermon in eight compartments was being developed, and that the shadow before me was that of one who was taking refuge from oratory in sleep.

Among the number of the shadows which my memory retains, there are some that lie upon it with no dark and shuddering chill; some that were cast by objects in themselves so pure and noble, that the shade itself seemed only a subdued brightness, and the light that cast it—a glory.

My story begins at the time, some years ago, when, as a single man, I was living in a narrow and rather crowded street, in one of the old parts of London—one of those streets where very decent houses are mixed with much poorer ones—and in one of the best and cleanest of which I occupied two rooms; a bed-room and a sitting-room. Having at that time, as I have now, a great dread of noise while at work, I made use of the back room as my studio, sleeping in the front of the house, which was quiet at night but not in the daytime, by reason of the day traffic. My painting-room, then, was on the second floor, and at the back of the house, and as there was a street running at an acute angle to that in which I lived, and joining it only a few yards higher up, it will easily be understood that the backs of the houses in this slanting thoroughfare, which was called, appropriately enough, Cross-street, were in tolerably close proximity to my painting-room window. I have been thus exact in describing the topography of my place of abode, because then you will be better able to understand how it happened that my attention was directed to the circumstances which I am about to detail.

You will be able to understand how it was, that, sitting, especially during the short days, as the dusk was beginning to fall, looking meditatively out of the window and thinking of my work, my attention would often be drawn, almost without my knowledge, to some of the windows in the slanting street which I have described, and how I found myself not unfrequently speculating about some of the inhabitants of the rooms which were separated from that in which I was sitting, by so small a space.

There was one window more than all the rest, which, for some reason or other, used especially to occupy my thoughts. It was a window exactly level with my own, and exactly opposite to it. During the daytime, though the blind was always drawn up as high as it could be, I could see but little of the room, but what I could make out only showed me that it was a very poor place indeed. Long habits of a speculative use of my eyes, if I may so express myself, have perhaps given me a tendency to attach much importance to the external aspects of things as indicative of what goes on within. Be that as it may, I possess that tendency, and possess it very strongly on the subject of windows. I think that the windows of a house give one a great idea of the dispositions, the habits, and the tempers of the occupants. Who has not felt, in passing by a house whose well-cleaned windows are filled with flowers,

where the solid white and green of the Arum, and the delicate shades of colour in the rows of blossoming hyacinths, stand out in pleasant freshness against the dark background formed by the interior of the room—who has not felt that the inhabitants of a house whose windows are thus decorated, are in a calmer and happier condition than their next-door neighbours, where the yellow blind hangs crookedly across the dirty window, and the wire screen beneath has got a bulging ragged hole in it?

Holding, then, the theory which I have ventured thus to put forward, it will be readily believed that I augured the better of the occupants of the room opposite, from the fact that I could see through the lower panes of the window the leaves and branches of a great big fuchsia spread out fan-wise on a wooden frame. Other little contrivances and adornments there were about this poor casement, which, though of the cheapest and most twopenny order of decorative art, showed yet some love of the gentler side of things, and a wish to put a good face on poverty.

But it is, as I have already said, towards dusk and in the evening that my attention has been oftenest fixed on the window which I have been describing. It is then that, the room being lighted up, the shadows of things and persons within it are thrown upon the blind with a clearness and distinctness which those who have never observed such matters would hardly credit. The shadows tell me, then, that the room is tenanted by a husband and wife, both young, I am certain. The man, as I gather from his position, and what I take to be the shadow of a tissue-paper screen behind which he stoops over his labour, is a poor drudging engraver for whom the days are not long enough, sitting cramped up at his patient toil through many hours of the night. As I watch him, he will rise and stretch back his head to relieve the muscles of his neck, and then I see that the shadow thrown on the blind is that of a young figure, spare but well made. The light shows me also that he wears a beard; it is a very strong light indeed, and this makes me more sure than ever that he is an engraver. The shadow of his wife is there beside him—almost always. How she watches over and tends him, how she hangs over his chair, or kneels beside him! I had never, at the time I speak of, seen her, but I could not help fancying that she was pretty and good enough to light up a darker room than that in which she lives, and to make her husband's life of toil—if he can keep it up—not only bearable but delightful.

If he can keep it up—but can he? His shadow is all that I have seen of him, but it looks like the shadow of one in delicate health. I never miss him from his place at night, and I can see the edge of his blind by which he works, at his window all day. "If he sits drudging there," thought I, "he will surely, as is the case in all excess, defeat his own object and end in being disabled altogether."

It was not long before I began to fear that what I had apprehended had taken place. There came a day when the blind was not drawn up to let in the light on the engraver's work, but remained drawn down the whole day. It would be difficult to express how anxiously I longed for the evening, and the shadows which should tell me more.

That evening the light was burning in the room as usual, but the straight edge of the engraver's blind was not seen cutting against it. There was the shadow of but one person, it was that of a woman, and as the figure which cast it moved so quietly about, I could make out that she was pouring out drugs and mixing the different compounds wanted in a sick-room by the light of the lamp. Sometimes she would pause in these occupations and look towards one end of the room, where I concluded the bed was placed; and sometimes I could even imagine, but this must have been pure fancy, that, looking still in the same direction, her lips would move at times, and that she was speaking. I could even see her tasting the food she was mixing, with her head a little on one side; altering and tasting it often before she carried it across the room to where I felt sure the sick man lay. So much will shadows tell.

From my front window I can see a long way up and down the street, even to that corner where the early breakfast depôt is found every morning—a poor stall enough, and driving a poor business, I should have thought; a business, however, in which I am so deeply interested that my first morning act is to go to the window and see if the poor old proprietor has got a customer—nay, once I put on a pilot-coat and a wideawake hat to appear in character, and purchased a cup of his coffee, which was a sound coffee enough, though a little gritty, and perhaps a thought weak. Enough of that. I can see to the coffee-stall one way, and nearly as far the other, and at the back I command a bit of a court, two mewses and a half, and, by great dislocation of neck, a little scrap of Brewer-street, Golden-square. Now in all these regions which are continually under my eye, I have noticed one constantly pervading presence, one figure which comes upon the scene without fail every day in the year, and at all conceivable hours. It is the figure of a tallish gentleman of about five-and-thirty, who stoops a little, has a very round back, wears spectacles, is always dressed in a buttoned black frock-coat, is always in a hurry, always expected anxiously at the houses he visits, and always followed to the door, on coming out again, by some who question him eagerly as he leaves them, and who seem to seek for comfort in his most inscrutable face. Of course I have not watched this gentleman's proceedings long, without coming to the conclusion that it is Mr. Cordial, the parish doctor, whose surgery in Great Pulteney-street I am so often in the habit of passing.

If there had been any previous doubt on my mind as to the state of things in the house opposite, it would at once have been put to flight when, on the day succeeding that evening on which I had watched the engraver's wife in her capacity of nurse, I caught a dark glimpse of this gentleman's head (rather a bald head for so young a man) at the window of the room opposite, which he had come to, to prepare some mixture or other.

"Now here," I thought to myself, "is a pretty business. This is just what I feared. Here is this poor fellow laid up, unable to work, and probably not only ill in body, but harassed in mind by the consciousness that as long as he is ill, there can be no money coming in to supply the daily expenses which, however poorly they live, he and his wife must of necessity incur."

I thought over this matter, and turned it all sorts of ways, as people who are unlucky enough or unwise enough, to live alone do turn and twist things, and was so haunted by the thought of what was going on in the room opposite, that in the course of the afternoon I was obliged to go out and take a long walk, in order to fill up the time that must necessarily intervene before the lamp would be lit, and the shadows thrown upon the blind. When I got back from that walk I was in such hot haste for such silent news as I might reasonably hope to gain, that I did not even stay to light my candle, but felt my way as well as I could across the room, and stationed myself at the window.

At first I thought that there were no shadows at all on the white glaring blind, except those of the poor bits of curtain and of the spread-out fuchsia before mentioned, but by-and-by, noticing a small and continually moving shadow, mixed up with that of the curtain, and observing that it rose and fell regularly and quickly, I presently connected it with another mass of shade a little above it, and arrived at the conclusion that this last was thrown by a woman's head, and by the moving shadow by her hand, as it rose and fell in the action of working with the needle. It was not long before I found out that my hypothesis was well grounded; for a little while the shadow of the hand was still and that of the head was raised, as if the person whose silhouette lay thus upon the blind was in the act of listening—and then it rose, and I saw the well-known figure of the engraver's wife pass the light, and knew that she had moved towards that quarter of the room in which I had made up my mind that the bed with the sick man in it was placed.

During the greater part of that evening, as I watched, and my occupations were frequently interrupted that I might do so, I made out no shadow but that which I have just mentioned. But, at about nine o'clock, I saw another shadow pass before the blind, and as it was that of a man, I had for a moment the hope that it was cast by the invalid. It was only for a moment; another glance showed me that this person wore no beard, and that there was greater bulk of figure than would have been cast by the poor engraver. I soon concluded that it was the doctor; and if I had any doubt on this subject it was removed when I presently observed the workman-like angle of elbow made by the shadow as it stood before the light, pouring something into what I suppose, from its size, must have been a teacup. Twice a day, then. He was ill enough for the doctor to come to him twice a day.

My determination was taken as I made that reflection. I had got wrought up to a great state of interest and suspense about this case which I could hardly explain to myself. I felt a strange longing to know more of it, and I came to the resolution—it was like what might have been ex-

pected of a man half-cracked with living alone—
that I would go out then and there, waylay the
doctor as he came away from his patient, and ask
him all about it.

I had lost some time in reflection, and when I
looked hastily across before leaving my room I
did not see any shadows on the blind, yet it was
reasonable to suppose that I might still catch the
doctor in the street; so out I rushed. Sure
enough, there was the doctor just coming out of
No. 4, Cross-street. How lucky I was to be in
time!

I found the parish medical authority not very
communicative or prone to take a very romantic
view of sickness and suffering. He was a good
sort of man enough, no doubt, but dry and matter-
of-fact. He had seen so much of sickness and
misery that he was used to it. He answered all
my questions, however, politely, though seeming
a good deal surprised at them.

"He had just been visiting a sick man in that
house, had he not?" I asked.

"Yes," he replied, "he had. Bad case of low
fever."

"Second floor—a married couple?" was my
next inquiry.

Again an answer in the affirmative.

"Was it a case of great distress?"

"Yes, of very great distress."

"They have nothing to live upon but what the
husband makes by his labour?" I asked.

"Nothing," was the answer.

"And he is laid up and unable to work?"

"That is the state of the case," replied the
doctor.

"Ah! I thought so," said I. "Would you be
kind enough, Doctor Cordial," I continued, "to
take charge of this small sum" (it was a very
small one) "for the benefit of these poor people—
on no account mentioning how you came by it."

The doctor promised that he would, and I was
just going to leave him, when I thought I would
ask the poor fellow's name.

"His name is Adams," said the doctor, and so
we parted.

I now felt quite a sense of proprietorship in
looking at my poor shadows opposite, and watched
them more eagerly than ever. There was one
action of the shadow, now unfortunately the only
action to watch, which used to puzzle me not a
little. The sick man's wife used at times to stand
before the light, and, as it appeared to me, used
to hold some article of clothing, or other piece of
drapery, and examine it closely; sometimes I
fancied that I could make the object out to be a
shirt, or a coat, at another time a pair of trousers.
After this she would disappear, and I always
noticed that the lamp would then be turned down
till its light was very low, and would remain so
for a considerable period. I could not understand
this at the time, though I did afterwards. She
was testing the condition of different articles of
clothing before taking them to the pawnbroker's.

And now I began to discover one of the bad
results of my solitary life. Though I had given
Doctor Cordial a small sum to go towards helping
these poor people, it was quite impossible, in my
straitened circumstances, that I could spare more.
If I had resolutely kept my friends about me,
there would have been somebody or other to
whom I could apply in behalf of my poor shadows,
while now it was impossible to do so. Even
when the idea entered my mind of trying to re-
vive some former friendships with this view, the
fear that any one so applied to might imagine I
wanted the help for myself, at once deterred me.

Whilst I was engaged in turning all these
things over in my mind, there came across it the
memory of one individual to whom I really felt as
if I should not mind applying in this difficulty.
This was a certain Mr. Pycroft, a copperplate
printer, with whom I had formerly had dealings. He
was an old man, and it so happened that at one
time in my life I had been in a position to do him
a service, and had done it. There was something
about his age, his position, and our former relations, which made me feel less shy of approaching
him than I should have felt with any one else.
He was a fat, jolly-looking old boy, and was, as
far as I had opportunities of judging, as good-
natured as he looked.

There was, however, one important circumstance
connected with his history which seemed to show
him in a less amiable light, and the remembrance
of which made me for a time hesitate about applying to him. I remembered to have heard that
some short time ago he had acted with great severity towards his eldest son, who, having contracted
a marriage against his father's wishes, had been
deprived of his share in the business, which he
had formerly enjoyed, and left to make a living as
well as he could by his own exertions. The fact
is, that the old man had had a darling project of
marrying his eldest son to a young girl whose
father was a business connexion of his own. The
old copper-plate printer was not only thwarted in
this, but was further outraged by his son's choice
having fallen in a direction particularly distasteful
to him for private reasons. I suspected also from
what I had heard, that the conduct of the eldest
son, which had been represented to his father as
being violent and rebellious in no ordinary degree,
had been made the worst of by the younger brother, who not only stepped into the lion's share
of the business on his brother's removal, but himself contracted the marriage which his brother
had declined. I could not help thinking when I
heard the circumstances of the case that this
younger son would have had a great deal to do in poison-
ing the old man's mind with regard to his elder
brother's conduct.

At all events, old Mr. Pycroft was the only person I could think of just now as likely to help my
unfortunate shadows, and to him I determined to
apply, but in a roundabout way. It occurred to
me that if I could enlist his sympathy in the fate
of these poor people, just as my own had been
awakened, by means of the shadows, it would be
a far better plan than any other.

It so happened that I had often promised my
old acquaintance to show him a collection which
I had of Rembrandt etchings, and it occurred to
me that now was the time when these might come
into play with great effect. So, making an excuse
in relation to the matter of business which had
formerly brought us together, I called on my old
acquaintance, and, in the course of conversation,
invited him, naming an evening, to come to my

lodgings, and examine these curiosities, intimating that we would moisten that pleasing labour with a glass of brandy-and-water. Punctual to the time named Mr. Pycroft arrived, and we got through the first hour very comfortably, though I could not help feeling rather anxious about the success of my scheme.

After examining the etchings, Mr. Pycroft, over the second glass, began to rally me about living in such a labyrinth of streets, asking me if I did not find it dreadfully confined at the back.

"By-the-by," I said—and here I must own that I was guilty of some small amount of deception, for I spoke as if the matter in hand were of no sort of importance—"by-the-by, Mr. Pycroft, you wouldn't imagine how much recreation I derive from observing my neighbours in that very cross street which you find comes too near my windows."

"If you was to come out of this kind of solitary life," replied Mr. P , "you would have other things to amuse yourself with besides the goings on of a parcel of people whom you know nothing about."

"Now here, for instance," I went on, unmindful of the interruption, as I drew aside my own curtain and pointed out the window of the room occupied by my poor young couple—"here is a window which has revealed to me all sorts of interesting matter—enough to make a story out of almost, I can tell you."

"What, this window opposite? But do you mean to say, Mr. B., that you think it right to look into people's rooms like that?"

"I have scrupulously abstained from doing so," was my answer, "and have made all my observations with the blind down, as you see it now."

"With the blind down? But how could you make any observations with the blind down?"

"By means of the shadows of the occupants of the apartment," was my answer.

"Shadows!" cried Mr. Pycroft, obviously incredulous. "You don't mean to tell me that you could make out what was going on in that room by means of the shadows on the blind?"

"Something of what goes on," I replied, "at any rate. Enough to interest me in the fortunes of those to whom the room belongs."

"Well, really Mr. B.! If I had it on any other testimony than your own I should have thought it simply impossible."

"Would you like to look for yourself?" I said. "I dare say something will take place behind the blind before long, which will give you an opportunity of testing the accuracy of what I have said."

"Well, without doubting that at all," replied my guest, "I really think I should."

Mr. Pycroft was sitting near the window, but my reading-lamp upon the table made the room rather too light for our observations. So I pushed the table away to the other end of the room, turned down the wick of the lamp, and lowered the shade over it as well.

"Well," said Mr. Pycroft, "I see nothing at present but a white blind with a light behind it."

The shadow of the little wife's head was there in the corner by the curtain, and the shadow of the hand rose and fell as usual; but Mr. Pycroft had not such a practised eye as I had for detecting

such matters. I pointed these out to my friend.

"I do see something bobbing up and down," he said, "now you mention it. But I should never have found it out without your help. Stop! there's a shadow now covering nearly the whole blind. What's that?"

"I suspect that it is the shadow of the same person." was my answer. "She will probably go nearer the window and farther from the light presently, and then you will see."

In a minute or two the shadow appeared again, and this time not so large.

"I can make it out now," said my friend, "quite easily : it is the shadow of a woman. I can see the line of the waist and of the skirts of the dress."

"Can you make out the face at all?" I asked.

"Oh yes," answered Mr. P. "It is turned sideways, looking to the left there. She's gone now," he added in a moment.

In a few minutes her shadow was thrown again upon the blind.

"What's she about now?" asked Mr. Pycroft.

"Nay, you shall tell me," I answered.

"Well, she seems to have some small object in her hand which she is shaking."

"And now?" I asked again.

"I can't make out, her elbow seems raised—both hands are raised. No, I can't make out at all."

"I think she is pouring something out," said I.

"So she is, no doubt," answered my guest, who was evidently becoming much interested. "Stay," he continued, after a moment's pause, and looking at me quite anxiously as he spoke—"shaking, pouring—'to be well shaken before taken'—why, it must be medicine."

"I suspect it is medicine," was my answer.

"Is there some one ill, then?" asked Mr. Pycroft.

"Yes," I replied, "her husband."

"And did the shadow tell you that, too?"

"Yes, the shadow of her husband used to appear on the blind as often as hers, now I never see it. Exactly coincident with the disappearance of the husband's shadow has been the arrival of another shadow, which has been that of the parish doctor."

"And pray," asked Mr. Pycroft with the air of one whose credulity had been really too much tasked at last, "may I ask how you knew it to be the doctor's shadow?"

"Doctor Cordial has the roundest back you ever saw in your life," was my answer.

"Well, this is really very curious," ejaculated the old copper-plate printer, who was now evidently powerfully interested.

As we continued to look, the light was suddenly removed, and the room was left in darkness.

"What do you suppose has happened now?" inquired my companion.

"I suppose," was my answer, "that she has left the room for a short time. We shall see more presently, no doubt;" and almost as I spoke the light reappeared, and another shadow was in the room besides that of the little wife.

"The doctor?" asked Mr. Pycroft.

"There," I cried, triumphantly, "you see how

much may be discovered by shadows. You are expert already."

"He *has* a round back, certainly," said the old copper-plate printer.

The round-backed shadow now faded off softly in the direction towards which the profile of the little wife was turned so often. The white blind remained for some minutes shadowless.

"I suppose he is examining his patient now," said Mr. Pycroft; "here he is again," he added in another minute. The doctor, however, stood so near the light this time and so completely with his back towards us, that we were unable to determine what he was doing. This was, naturally, often the case with the shadows. Much as one was able to make out, there was, of course, infinitely more, an explanation of which it was impossible even to guess at.

In a short time the round-backed shadow was joined by that of the sick man's wife, and then the two stood for some time in conversation; at least it was reasonable to suppose so.

"Giving her directions, I shouldn't wonder," said the copper-plate printer.

"Most likely," I answered.

"I wonder if he's *very* bad," said my companion. After this there was a pause. The two shadows continued standing by the table. At last, we both thought that the doctor's shadow appeared to give something to the shade of the engraver's wife, and immediately after, the light was removed as it had been before: it had been probably taken out on to the landing in order that the doctor might see his way down stairs.

"And so they're very poor," said Mr. Pycroft, as if talking to himself.

"They had nothing but what the husband could earn," I answered, "and he is wholly incapable of working, and will remain so probably for weeks to come."

The light had now reappeared in the room. The shadow of the little wife seemed to linger by the table after setting it down. Her figure was motionless for a considerable time, and then we noted that the head fell forward, and that the face was buried in the hands as if in an agony of silent grief.

We neither of us spoke, and at the same moment I dropped the curtain of my own window which had before been fastened back, for I felt that this was sorrow with which a spectator had no right to intermeddle.

Soon afterwards my old friend rose to go, and we spoke not another word on the matter. Just before I retired to rest, however, I looked out once more. The shadow of the little wife's head was in its usual place, and the shadow of her hand rose and fell as usual. She was at work again.

The next day, by an early post, I received a letter from Mr. Pycroft. He had been thinking a great deal, he said, of what he had seen the night before, and enclosed a little money, which he asked me to see applied to the benefit of the young couple in whose fortunes I had interested myself. He also begged me from time to time to let me have tidings of what "the shadows" were about.

I handed the money over to Dr. Cordial, asking him to apply it as might seem best to his judg-

ment, but making no mention of who it came from. I asked him also to let me have news as frequently as possible of the condition of his patient. These I transmitted pretty nearly as often as I received them to the old copper-plate printer.

For some days there was not much to report, nor did the shadows tell me anything different from what they had before revealed. The poor engraver's shadow was still wanting, and that of his little wife was either stationary in the corner, when she did what she could to earn a little money with her needle, or else was seen flitting about the room in attendance on her sick husband. At length there came a time when the fever reached its crisis, and when it was clear, according to the doctor's report, that the sufferer must sink under it or recover. To make my story as short as possible, I will not dwell on the details of this period of suspense. The one quality of youth, possessed by the patient, enabled his constitution to rally, and after this crisis in his disorder he began to mend.

And now a long convalescence followed, and a time arrived when one evening the shadow of a wasted figure moved slowly past the light, and I could guess as I watched it, and observed that it was accompanied by the well-known shadow of the little wife, that the sick man was moving from his bed to a chair by the fire.

Of course I made this advance known to my friend, the copper-plate printer, and kept him well acquainted with all the particulars of the gradual improvement in our invalid's health, even to the period when it was so far re-established that he was able at last to sit up for a certain number of hours every day at his engraving table, and work once more for his wife's support.

"They are very grateful," I said, when I made this announcement to my old acquaintance, "to the unknown friend who has assisted them from time to time throughout their trouble."

"Oh no, nonsense, nonsense; it's nothing, nothing at all—nothing at all," ejaculated the old fellow, trying to get away from the subject.

"And they are very anxious," I continued, resolutely, "to thank him personally, if he would but reveal himself and give them the opportunity."

"No, no, not for the world," was the answer; "oh dear no, impossible. Here, here's a little trifle extra just to set them going you know, because he mustn't work too much at first."

"And you won't let them see you?" I asked again.

"No, no, no, on no account," said the old boy. "I'll tell you what, though," he continued in a moment, "I should like to see *them*—see them as I did before—the shadows you know," he added. "I'll come and have a glass of brandy-and-water with you some evening, and have a look at the shadows again."

I was obliged to be satisfied with this, and making an engagement with my old friend for an early day, I left him, and went home.

The evening came, and with it an unusual amount of stir and bustle in the quiet room opposite. The figure of the little wife was continually flitting backwards and forwards in front of the light, as if she were engaged in smartening up the poor apartment. Hanging in the very middle of the window, and so close to the thin white blind that I could see it distinctly, there was a birdcage with a bird in it; and it was owing to the presence of this object that I had been chiefly able to form some idea of what my two friends opposite were like. When either of them approached the birdcage, as would sometimes happen, to give a chirp of encouragement to its occupant, I could see the profile of the person who did so, as distinctly as one used to trace the silhouettes of the old black portraits which itinerant artists were wont to cut out at fairs. Except at such times as this, when the engraver or his wife stood near the window and far from the light, I could distinguish little but a shapeless mass; and when either of them approached the candle nearly, their shadows became so gigantic that the whole space of the window—an unusually large one—was completely darkened, even by one figure. I must repeat what I have said before, that the opportunities were very rare when I could make out what the shadows were about, and that in all cases in which I could detect such processes of mixing drinks, pouring out of medicines, and the like, it was owing to the fact that some necessary object connected with the proceeding was placed on some article of furniture which stood in or near the window.

Punctual to the appointed time, my old friend, the copper-plate printer, made his appearance, and his first question after the usual greeting had been exchanged, was:

"Well—how are the shadows?"

I placed his chair in the old position, and we both sat down.

The bustle and movement to which I have adverted as going on in the room opposite, were still noticeable, and I had little doubt that the apartment was being " cleaned up;" an impression to which additional force was soon given by the dawning on the scene of a thin, straight shadow, which I took to be a broomstick, and which was now brought into active service.

I must not omit to mention, that at the moment of a certain pause in the career of the broom, the figure of the poor engraver was thrown with great distinctness on the blind. He had come to the window to stick some object, probably a piece of groundsel, between the wires of the birdcage.

When this happened, I noticed a great change come over the countenance of my guest. He raised himself in his chair, and looking eagerly forward, said, in quite a strange tone of voice:

"What did you say was the name of these people?"

"Adams," was my answer.

"Adams,—you are quite sure."

"Quite," I replied. By this time the shadow had vanished again, but I remarked that for a considerable time Mr. Pycroft seemed absent and uncomfortable, and we talked of many matters foreign to the subject I had at heart, before he again returned to the shadows.

"They seem quiet enough now," said Mr. Pycroft at last.

"I dare say," I answered, "that the cleaning of the room is over, and that they have sat down to a bit of supper."

"Do you think so?" said the old copper-plate printer.

" I dare say they have some little luxury, furnished by your liberality."

"Do you really think so?" said the old boy, who had a great idea of comfort. "What do you think they've got? I wish the shadows would show us that!"

I darted at once at the opening which I saw here.

"The shadows will not show it," I said; "but why not go across and see the substance? It would make their supper all the sweeter to them, I am sure."

The old gentleman had just finished a tumbler of hot grog. He was in high good humour, and as I finished speaking his eyes began to twinkle, and a latent smile developed itself about the corners of his mouth.

"It wouldn't be bad fun, would it?" he said.

I wanted nothing more, and in another minute he was on his legs, and we were on our way to No. 4.

A little girl was on the door-step with a pot of beer in her hand, and we had no sooner stopped before the house than she made known a want incidental to the lives of maidens who stand only three feet two inches in their stockings:

"Please, sir, will you ring the second bell from the top?"

"Second floor?" I said, as I complied; "that's where Mr. and Mrs. Adams live, isn't it?"

"Yes, sir, and he's my father," said the young lady, who evidently looked upon the couple alluded to as one flesh. I thought it odd I had never seen this child's shadow on the blind.

"Well, I want to see him, then," I replied, "and so does this gentleman."

"Oh, but you can't, though," said the little girl, who, by the way, appeared to be a precocious shrew—"for father's at supper, and there's a fowl, and father's been ill, and you can't disturb him just as he's a little better—so that you can't."

"You just hold your tongue, miss, will you?" said a voice at this juncture, "and let me talk to the gentleman."

I looked up and saw that the door had been opened by a tall gaunt-looking woman, with a large nose.

"Who did you please to want, sir?" she asked in a whining tone, which I disliked very much.

I told her briefly who we were, and the object of our visit.

"Oh, what a joyful surprise!" said the gaunt woman, whining as before in a manner infinitely offensive to me. "Get along up-stairs, Lizzy," she continued, addressing the child, "and tell your father that the kind gentleman as assisted him in his illness is coming to see him; I'm his wife, kind gentlemen"—(*this* the shadow that I had interested myself in!)—"I'm his poor wife that nussed him through his illness, and—take care of the stairs, kind gentlemen—and this is the room, gentlemen; and here's a joyful surprise, James; the gentlemen that's been so kind all the time you've been ill; and be pleased to take a seat, gentlemen, and honour our poor room by sitting down in it."

I was thunderstruck. A little common-looking

man was sitting at the table on which a smoking fowl, a bit of bacon, and some potatoes had been placed. He bore the evident marks of recent illness, and rose with some effort at our entry. He resumed his seat, however, as I and my companion sat down. I took a chair, as I should have taken anything that was offered me in sheer surprise and bewilderment. I looked once more at the man's wife. What, was that the substance of the 'neat little shadow which I knew so well—that great gaunt sloping creature? Were shadows so deceptive as this? Would anybody tell me that my opposite neighbour could have had such a nose as I now saw, and that it would not have stood out in bold relief and left its mark upon my memory every time she approached the window?

The husband, too. That was not my poor engraver. He was an inoffensive man enough, as he sat there full of clumsy expressions of gratitude to my companion for the assistance accorded to him during his recent attack of fever. He was a harmless little man, no doubt. Not quite such a heavy blow as his wife; but still, he was not my engraver.

All this time, even while her husband was speaking, the gaunt woman kept up an undercurrent of gratitude of the slimiest description, to which the old gentleman answered not a word, for he seemed as little prepared for the real Mr. and Mrs. Adams by what he had seen of their shadows as I was. In short, beyond a few words of inquiry as to the state of the invalid's health, which I had managed to utter on first coming into the room, we had neither of us spoken a word.

Suddenly the tremendous idea entered my mind that there must be some mistake. I had been staring some time at the little girl whom we originally met on the door-step, and who, to do her justice, returned the compliment with interest, when it struck me that her head came considerably above the window-sill, and that consequently, it was a most extraordinary thing that its shadow had never caught my attention. My eyes having in the course of this comparison of the young lady with the window-sill been directed towards this last part of the room, I next observed that there was no birdcage hanging in the window.

"Halloa!" I ejaculated, "you've taken down the birdcage."

"Birdcage, sir?" whined the gaunt woman, deferentially.

"We ain't got no birdcage," burst out the small child of the door-step, "nor never haven't had none—nor yet no bird neither."

"Will you hold your tongue, miss?" interposed her mother.

There was an awkward pause. I looked again about the room, I looked at the woman, I looked at her husband—he had no beard, I now observed. I had, however, presence of mind enough not to ask after that missing appendage as I had done after the birdcage. I determined to make assurance doubly sure, and walking towards the window and pulling aside the blind, observed, as an excuse for looking out:

"I am afraid you must be a good deal choked up at the back with houses. Isn't that rather unwholesome?"

A voluble answer on the subject of confined lodgings, their advantages and disadvantages, followed, but I did not hear it. I was looking for my own window in the house opposite. I had left the lamp alight and the blind half drawn up. The window before me, exactly in front of that which I was looking from, was fastened up and secured with shutters. Stretching my neck, and glancing in a slanting direction towards the next of the opposite houses, I saw that the second-floor window was illuminated, and that the blind was half lowered.

"Your supper is getting cold," I said, coming back to the table, and exchanging a glance of meaning with my companion; "my friend and I only wished to come in and see how you were enjoying yourselves, and so now we will leave you to do better justice to the fowl than you could if we remained here."

So saying, and resisting all entreaties to stay and take a share of the good things, I made for the door, and was soon on the staircase, followed closely by Mr. Pycroft, who, speechless as long as we remained in the room, did nothing now but repeat, "Wrong people, eh?—been feeding the wrong people, haven't we?" in a loud and perfectly audible whisper. The gaunt woman was, however, too loquacious herself to hear what was said, and during the time that she lighted us down the stairs, never ceased whining out her gratitude for a single moment.

When we got into the street I turned round and looked my companion in the face.

"It is some comfort, at any rate," I said, "to think that you have been assisting people who were really in need of help, but it is evident that every penny of your bounty has gone to the family we have just left."

"And how do you account for the mistake?" asked my old friend.

"I can only conclude," was my answer, "that by a curious coincidence there have been two second-floor lodgers ill in two houses next door to each other; that after my seeing Dr. Cordial at the window opposite to mine, he had gone from the one house to the other; that he had had time to pay a short visit to the invalid we have just left; and that then I had met him coming away, as I thought, from attending on our poor shadows, but in reality from the deserving personage whose supper has been supplied by your benevolence."

"And the shadows?" gasped Mr. Pycroft, utterly aghast.

"Have, through my unfortunate mistake, not received a single shilling," was my answer.

Mr. Pycroft stared at me for some time in petrified amazement.

"We can never leave the thing like this," he said, at last. "Do you think you could be sure of the house this time?"

"I can understand your feeling some mistrust about it," I said, "but I own that I feel none myself. This is the house beyond a doubt" I looked up as I spoke at No. 5.

"Then let's bring the matter to a conclusion at once," said the old copper-plate printer, stoutly; and with that we actually rang at the second bell handle on the left hand door-post.

After the proper amount of delay the door was opened by a slatternly woman.

"Second-floor back?" said I in a mellifluous voice.

"Front," replied the slatternly woman, in rather an injured tone; "you should have rung the bell on the right door-post."

I begged pardon with all humility, and the slatternly woman relented a little.

"The two-pair-back's at home, I know," she said, "and if you're coming up, I may as well light you."

We availed ourselves of this offer, and, in a few seconds, we were on the second-floor landing. The slatternly woman pointed out the door at which we were to knock, and opening her own, and letting out in so doing a blast of onions that almost made my eyes water, she disappeared into the refreshing vapour, and shut herself in with it.

My curiosity was now powerfully piqued, and I felt as if some great stake hinged upon the opening of the door at which we stood and knocked.

A clear, cheerful voice called to us to enter, and in another moment we stood inside the room. Two people, a man and a woman, occupied the apartment. One of them, the man, was at first hidden from view, but in the other, as she rose upon our entrance, I recognised at once the shadow with which I was so familiar.

The room was a great contrast to that which we had just left, which was tolerably well provided with furniture. This room was utterly bare, looking as if all available objects had been removed, as probably they had, to be turned into money. A mattress and some bedding were on the floor at one end of the room. The table, and a couple of old chairs, were the only articles of furniture I could see. The engraver's lamp was on the table, and the materials for a very poor meal which the two had evidently just been cooking—a very little scrap of bacon and some boiled rice. The birdcage was hanging in the window, if I had wanted any confirmation of my conviction that I had found my shadows at last.

Of course, all these things were taken in by me at a single glance, it being necessary that I should at once account for my visit and that of my friend. I had begun to do so in a few hurried words, when my attention was suddenly arrested by an exclamation from Mr. Pycroft, who had followed me. The second occupant of the room, whom we had at first seen but imperfectly, had now risen to his feet, and stood with the light full upon him, straining his eyes into the shade where my companion stood behind me. I turned hastily round, and met the stern gaze of my old friend.

"If this is a trick, Mr. Broadhead," he said, speaking very thick, and with choking utterance, "I can tell you that it does you little credit."

"What do you mean?" I asked, in utter bewilderment.

"I mean that if this has all been a planned thing to bring about a reconciliation between me and my son——"

"Your son?" I gasped.

"I can only say," continued Mr. Pycroft, "that it shall meet with the success it deserves."

He turned as he spoke and made for the door, but I was beforehand with him.

"Stay, Mr. Pycroft!" I cried. "If you choose to retain this feeling of animosity, which so ill becomes you, you must, but you shall not go away with a false impression of this matter as far as I am concerned in it. I swear to you that your suspicions of me are false, that when we came to this room I had no more idea of who were its occupants than you had, and that I never knew your son was living in this abject misery; though, if I had, I would certainly have done my best to rouse you to a feeling of what, under such circumstances, you owe to one who bears your name."

Mr. Pycroft had glanced once searchingly towards me when I denied his imputation of having been concerned in a plot to trick him into a reconciliation, and now his eyes were directed towards the place where his son stood before him.

He was a fine manly-looking fellow, and as he stood there holding his wife's hand in his, and with the refining influence of recent illness showing on his worn but handsome face, I could not help feeling that surely this picture must complete the work which the shadows had so well begun.

"Look at them!" I said—"Look at this room—look at that meal! Can you see such wretchedness and not be moved? If your son has displeased you has he not suffered? If he has disobeyed, he has paid the penalty."

I looked in my companion's face, and I thought that I saw some shadow of compunction working there.

"Do not," I said, "let the sympathy which you bestowed upon the shadows be wanting for the realities which cast them."

The little wife at this moment left her husband's side, and, advancing to where we stood, laid her hand timidly on that of my old friend. I looked at him once more, and then, beckoning the poor engraver to his father's side, I passed quietly from the room, where I felt that my presence was no longer needed.

About an hour afterwards, I was sitting disconsolately in my room, reflecting on the loneliness of my own position, and rather envying my opposite neighbours, when I heard my own name shouted in a cheery voice from without.

I looked in the old direction, and saw my friend Mr. Pycroft standing at his son's open window.

"We want you to come over," said the old gentleman, "and spend what is left of the evening with us."

I assented gladly, and was just drawing in my head, when I heard myself called once more by name.

"And I say," said Mr. Pycroft, in a stage whisper, "as we are rather short of liquor here, perhaps you wouldn't mind bringing a bottle of brandy in your pocket; and if you happen to have such a thing as a lemon——"

In a few minutes I was sitting one of a comfortable party in the room opposite.

"Do you know what is one of the first things we intend to do now?" said the little wife, smiling as she looked at me.

"I have not the least idea," was my answer.

"Why, we are going to nail up the thickest curtain we can get, in order to prevent our opposite neighbour from seeing what we are about whenever our lamp happens to be alight."

"You need not be afraid," I said; "and you may save yourself the trouble of putting up the curtain, for the opposite neighbour hopes henceforth to see so much of his new friends in their Substance, that he is not likely to trouble himself much more about—their Shadows."

-------- ◆ --------

III.

PICKING UP TERRIBLE COMPANY.

WHILE the artist was still engaged in telling his story, another visitor had come in at the gate, and had politely remained in the background, so as not to interrupt the proceedings. When the story was over, he came forward, and presented himself (in excellent English) as a Frenchman on a visit to this country. In the course of an eventful life, opportunities had occurred to him of learning our language, on the Continent, and necessity had obliged him to turn them to good account. Many years had passed, since that time, and had allowed him no earlier chance of visiting England than the chance of which he had now availed himself. He was staying with some friends in the neighbourhood—the Hermit had been mentioned to him—and here he was, on the ground of Thomas Tiddler, to deposit his homage at the feet of that illustrious landed proprietor.

Was the French visitor surprised? Not the least in the world. His face showed deep marks of former care and trouble—perhaps he was past feeling surprised at anything? By no means. If he had seen Mr. Mopes on French ground, he would have been petrified on the spot. But Mr. Mopes on English ground was only a new development of the dismal national character. Given British spleen, as the cause—followed British suicide, as the effect. Quick suicide (of which the works of his literary countrymen had already informed him) by throwing yourself into the water. Slow suicide (of which his own eyes now informed him) by burying yourself among soot and cinders, in a barred kitchen. Curious either way—but nothing to surprise a well-read Frenchman.

Leaving our national character to assert itself to better advantage, when time had given this gentleman better opportunities of studying it, Mr. Traveller politely requested him to follow the relation of the artist's experience with an experience of his own. After a moment's grave consideration, the Frenchman said that his early life had been marked by perils and sufferings of no ordinary kind. He had no objection to relate one of his adventures—but he warned his audience beforehand that they must expect to be a little startled; and he begged that they would suspend their opinions of himself and

his conduct, until they had heard him to the end.

After those prefatory words, he began as follows:

I AM a Frenchman by birth, and my name is François Thierry. I need not weary you with my early history. Enough, that I committed a political offence—that I was sent to the galleys for it—that I am an exile for it to this day. The brand was not abolished in my time. If I chose, I could show you the fiery letters on my shoulder.

I was arrested, tried, and sentenced, in Paris. I went out of the court with my condemnation ringing in my ears. The rumbling wheels of the prison-van repeated it all the way from Paris to Bicêtre that evening, and all the next day, and the next, and the next, along the weary road from Bicêtre to Toulon. When I look back upon that time, I think I must have been stupified by the unexpected severity of my sentence; for I remember nothing of the journey, nor of the places where we stopped—nothing but the eternal repetition of travaux forcés—travaux forcés—travaux forcés à perpétuité," over and over, and over again. Late in the afternoon of the third day, the van stopped, the door was thrown open, and I was conducted across a stone yard, though a stone corridor, into a huge stone hall, dimly lighted from above. Here I was interrogated by a military superintendent, and entered by name in a ponderous ledger bound and clasped with iron, like a book in fetters.

"Number Two Hundred and Seven," said the superintendent. "Green."

They took me into an adjoining room, searched, stripped, and plunged me into a cold bath. When I came out of the bath, I put on the livery of the galleys—a coarse canvas shirt, trousers of tawny serge, a red serge blouse, and heavy shoes clamped with iron. Last of all, a green woollen cap. On each leg of the trousers, and on the breast and back of the blouse, were printed the fatal letters "T. F." On a brass label in the front of the cap, were engraved the figures "207." From that moment I lost my individuality. I was no longer François Thierry. I was Number Two Hundred and Seven. The superintendent stood by and looked on.

"Come, be quick," said he, twirling his long moustache between his thumb and forefinger. "It grows late, and you must be married before supper."

"Married!" I repeated.

The superintendent laughed, and lighted a cigar, and his laugh was echoed by the guards and jailers.

Down another stone corridor, across another yard, into another gloomy hall, the very counterpart of the last, but filled with squalid figures, noisy with the clank of fetters, and pierced at each end with a circular opening, through which a cannon's mouth showed grimly.

"Bring Number Two Hundred and Six," said the superintendent, "and call the priest."

"Number Two Hundred and Six came from a farther corner of the hall, dragging a heavy chain, and along with him a blacksmith, bare-armed and leather-aproned.

"Lie down," said the blacksmith, with an insulting spurn of the foot.

I lay down. A heavy iron ring attached to a chain of eighteen links was then fitted to my ankle, and riveted with a single stroke of the hammer. A second ring next received the disengaged ends of my companion's chain and mine, and was secured in the same manner. The echo of each blow resounded through the vaulted roof like a hollow laugh.

"Good," said the superintendent, drawing a small red book from his pocket. "Number Two Hundred and Seven, attend to the prison code. If you attempt to escape without succeeding, you will be bastinadoed. If you succeed in getting beyond the port, and are then taken, you will receive three years of double-chaining. As soon as you are missed, three cannon shots will be fired, and alarm flags will be hoisted on every bastion. Signals will be telegraphed to the maritime guards, and to the police of the ten neighbouring districts. A price will be set upon your head. Placards will be posted upon the gates of Toulon, and sent to every town throughout the empire. It will be lawful to fire upon you, if you cannot be captured alive."

Having read this with grim complacency, the superintendent resumed his cigar, replaced the book in his pocket, and walked away.

All was over now—all the incredulous wonder, the dreamy dulness, the smouldering hope, of the past three days. I was a felon, and (slavery in slavery!) chained to a fellow-felon. I looked up, and found his eyes upon me. He was a swart heavy-browed sullen-jawed man of about forty; not much taller than myself, but of immensely powerful build.

"So," said he, "you're for life, are you? So am I."

"How do you know I am for life?" I asked, wearily.

"By that." And he touched my cap roughly with the back of his hand. "Green, for life. Red, for a term of years. What are you in for?"

"I conspired against the government."

He shrugged his shoulders contemptuously.

"Devil's mass! Then you are a gentleman-convict, I suppose! Pity you've not a berth to yourselves—we poor forçats hate such fine company."

"Are there many political prisoners?" I asked, after a moment's pause.

"None, in this department."

Then, as if detecting my unspoken thought, "I am no innocent," he added with an oath. "This is the fourth time I have been here. Did you ever hear of Gasparo?"

"Gasparo the forger?"

He nodded.

"Who escaped three or four months since, and—"

"And flung the sentinel over the ramparts, just as he was going to give the alarm. I am the man."

I had heard of him, as a man who, early in his career, had been sentenced to a long solitary imprisonment in a gloomy cell, and who had come forth from his solitude hardened into an absolute wild beast. I shuddered, and, as I shuddered, found his evil eye taking vindictive note of me. From that moment he hated me. From that moment I loathed him.

A bell rang, and a detachment of convicts came in from labour. They were immediately searched by the guard, and chained up, two and two, to a slooping wooden platform that reached all down the centre of the hall. Our afternoon meal was then served out, consisting of a mess of beans, an allowance of bread and ship-biscuit, and a measure of thin wine. I drank the wine; but I could eat nothing. Gasparo took what he chose from my untouched allowance, and those who were nearest, scrambled for the rest. The supper over, a shrill whistle echoed down the hall, each man took his narrow mattress from under the platform which made our common bedstead, rolled himself in a piece of seaweed matting, and lay down for the night. In less than five minutes, all was profoundly silent. Now and then I heard the blacksmith going round with his hammer, testing the gratings, and trying the locks, in all the corridors. Now and then, the guard stalked past with his musket on his shoulder. Sometimes, a convict moaned, or shook his fetters in his sleep. Thus the weary hours went by. My companion slept heavily, and even I lost consciousness at last.

I was sentenced to hard labour. At Toulon the hard labour is of various kinds; such as quarrying, mining, pumping in the docks, lading and unlading vessels, transporting ammunition, and so forth. Gasparo and I were employed with about two hundred other convicts in a quarry a little beyond the port. Day after day, week after week, from seven in the morning until seven at night, the rocks echoed with our blows. At every blow, our chains rang and rebounded on the stony soil. In that fierce climate, terrible tempests and tropical droughts succeed each other throughout the summer and autumn. Often and often, after toiling for hours under a burning sky, have I gone back to prison and to my pallet, drenched to the skin. Thus the last days of the dreary spring ebbed slowly past; and then the more dreary summer, and then the autumn-time, came round.

My fellow-convict was a Piedmontese. He had been a burglar, a forger, an incendiary. In his last escape, he had committed manslaughter. Heaven alone knows how my sufferings were muliplied by that abhorred companionship—how I shrank from the touch of his hand—how I sickened, if his breath came over me as we lay side by side at night. I strove to disguise my loathing; but in vain. He knew it as well as I knew it, and he revenged himself upon me by every means that a vindictive nature could devise. That he should tyrannise over me was not wonderful; for his physical strength was gigantic, and he was looked upon as an authorised despot throughout the port; but simple tyranny was the least part of what I had to endure. I had been fastidiously nurtured; he purposely and continually offended my sense of delicacy. I was unaccustomed to bodily labour; he imposed on me the largest share of our daily work. When I needed rest, he would insist on

2

walking. When my limbs were cramped, he would lie down obstinately, and refuse to stir. He delighted to sing blasphemous songs, and relate hideous stories of what he had thought and resolved on in his solitude. He would even twist the chain in such wise that it should gall me at every step. I was at that time just twenty-two years of age, and had been sickly from boyhood. To retaliate, or to defend myself, would have been alike impossible. To complain to the superintendent, would only have been to provoke my tyrant to greater cruelty.

There came a day. at length, when his hatred seemed to abate. He allowed me to rest when our hour of repose came round. He abstained from singing the songs I abhorred, and fell into long fits of abstraction. The next morning, shortly after we had begun work, he drew near enough to speak to me in a whisper.

"François, have you a mind to escape ?"

I felt the blood rush to my face. I clasped my hands. I could not speak.

"Can you keep a secret ?"

"To the death."

"Listen, then. To morrow, a renowned marshal will visit the port. He will inspect the docks, the prisons, the quarries. There will be plenty of cannonading from the forts and the shipping, and if two convicts escape, a volley more or less will attract no attention round about Toulon. Do you understand ?"

"You mean that no one will recognise the signals ?"

"Not even the sentries at the town-gates—not even the guards in the next quarry. Devil's mass ! What can be easier than to strike off each other's fetters with the pickaxe when the superintendent is not looking, and the salutes are firing ? Will you venture ?"

"With my life !"

"A bargain. Shake hands on it."

I had never touched his hand in fellowship before, and I felt as if my own were bloodstained by the contact. I knew by the sullen fire in his glance, that he interpreted my faltering touch aright.

We were roused an hour earlier than usual the following morning, and went through a general inspection in the prison-yard. Before going to work, we were served with a double allowance of wine. At one o'clock, we heard the first far-off salutes from the ships of war in the harbour. The sound ran through me like a galvanic shock. One by one, the forts took up the signal. It was repeated by the gun-boats closer in shore. Discharge followed discharge, all along the batteries on both sides of the port, and the air grew thick with smoke.

"As the first shot is fired yonder," whispered Gasparo, pointing to the barracks behind the prison, "strike at the first link of my chain, close to the ankle."

A rapid suspicion flashed across me.

"If I do, how can I be sure that you will free me afterwards? No, Gasparo; you must deal the first blow."

"As you please," he replied, with a laugh and an imprecation.

At the same instant, came a flash from the battlements of the barrack close by, and then a thunderous reverberation, multiplied again and again by the rocks around. As the roar burst over our heads, I saw him strike, and felt the fetters fall. Scarcely had the echo of the first gun died away, when the second was fired It was now Gasparo's turn to be free. I struck ; but less skilfully, and had twice to repeat the blow before breaking the stubborn link. We then went on, apparently. with our work, standing somewhat close together, with the chain huddled up between us. No one had observed us, and no one, at first sight, could have detected what we had done. At the third shot, a party of officers and gentlemen made their appearance at the bend of the road leading up to the quarry. In an instant, every head was turned in their direction ; every felon paused in his work ; every guard presented arms. At that moment we flung away our caps and pickaxes, scaled the rugged bit of cliff on which we had been toiling, dropped into the ravine below, and made for the mountain passes that lead into the valley. Encumbered still with the iron ankles to which our chains had been fastened, we could not run very swiftly. To add to our difficulties, the road was uneven, strewn with flints and blocks of fallen granite, and tortuous as the windings of a snake. Suddenly, on turning a sharp angle of projecting cliff, we came upon a little guard-house and a couple of sentries. To retreat was impossible. The soldiers were within a few yards of us. They presented their pieces, and called to us to surrender. Gasparo turned upon me like a wolf at bay.

"Curse you !" said he, dealing me a tremendous blow. "stay and be taken ! I have always hated you !"

I fell, as if struck down by a sledge hammer, and, as I fell, saw him dash one soldier to the ground, dart past the other, heard a shot, and then . . . all became dark, and I know no more.

When I next opened my eyes, I found myself lying on the floor of a small unfurnished room, dimly lighted by a tiny window close against the ceiling. It seemed as if weeks had gone by, since I lost consciousness. I had scarcely strength to rise, and, having risen, kept my feet with difficulty. Where my head had lain, the floor was wet with blood. Giddy and perplexed, I leaned against the wall, and tried to think.

In the first place, where was I ? Evidently in no part of the prison from which I had escaped. There, all was solid stone and iron grating ; here, was only whitewashed lath and plaster. I must be in a chamber of the little guard-house : probably in an upper chamber. Where, then, were the soldiers? Where was Gasparo ? Had I strength to clamber up to that window, and if so, in what direction did that window look oat? I stole to the door, and found it locked. I listened, breathlessly, but could hear no sound either below or above. Creeping back again, I saw that the little window was at least four feet above my head. The smooth plaster offered no projections by which I could raise myself, and there was not even a fireplace in the room from which I could have wrenched a bar to dig out holes in the wall for my feet and hands. Stay ! There was my leathern belt, and on the belt, the iron hook which used to sustain my chain when I was at work. I tore off the hook, picked away the lath and plaster in three or four places, climbed up, opened the window, and gazed out eagerly. Before me, at a distance of not more than thirty-five or forty feet, rose the rugged cliff under whose shelter the guard-house was built; at my feet, lay a little kitchen-garden, divided from the base of the rock by a muddy ditch which seemed to run through the ravine; to the right and left, as well as I could judge, lay the rocky path along which our course had been directed. My decision was taken at once. To stay was certain capture; to venture, at all hazards, would make matters no worse. Again I listened, and again all was quiet I drew myself through the little casement, dropped as gently as I could upon the moist earth, and, crouching against the wall, asked myself what I should do next. To climb the cliff would be to offer myself as a target to the first soldier who saw me. To venture along the ravine would be, perhaps, to encounter Gasparo and his captors face to face. Besides, it was getting dusk, and, under cover of the night, if I could only conceal myself till then, I might yet escape. But where was that concealment to be found? Heaven be thanked for the thought! There was the ditch.

Only two windows looked out upon the garden from the back of the guard-house. From one of those windows I had just now let myself down, and the other was partly shuttered up. I did not dare, however, openly to cross the garden. I dropped upon my face, and crawled in the furrows between the rows of vegetables, until I came to the ditch. Here, the water rose nearly to my waist, but the banks on either side were considerably higher, and, by stooping, I found that I could walk without bringing my head to the level of the road. I thus followed the course of the ditch for some two or three hundred yards in the direction of Toulon, thinking that my pursuers would be less likely to suspect me of doubling back towards prison, than of pushing forward towards the country. Half lying, half crouching under the rank grasses that fringed the bank above, I then watched the gathering shadows. By-and by I heard the evening gun, and a moment after, something like a distant sound of voices. Hark! was that a shout? Unable to endure the agony of suspense, I lifted my head, and peeped cautiously out. There were lights moving in the windows of the guard-house—there were dark figures in the garden—there were hasty tramplings of feet upon the road above! Presently a light flashed over the water only a few yards from my hiding-place! I slid gently down at full length, and suffered the foul ooze to close noiselessly over me. Lying thus, I held my breath till the very beatings of my heart seemed to suffocate me, and the veins in my temples were almost bursting. I could bear it no longer—I rose to the surface—I breathed again—I looked—I listened. All was darkness and silence. My pursuers were gone by!

I suffered an hour to go by, too, before I ventured to move again. By that time it was intensely dark, and had begun to rain heavily. The water in the ditch became a brawling torrent, through which I waded, unheard, past the very windows of the guard-house.

After toiling through the water for a mile or more, I ventured out upon the road again: and so, with the rain and wind beating in my face, and the scattered boulders tripping me up continually, I made my way through the whole length of the winding pass, and came out upon the more open country about midnight. With no other guide than the wind, which was blowing from the north-east, and without even a star to help me, I then struck off to the right, following what seemed to be a rough by-road, lying through a valley. By-and-by the rain abated, and I discerned the dark outlines of a chain of hills extending all along to the left of the road. These, I concluded, must be the Maures. All was well, so far. I had taken the right direction, and was on the way to Italy.

Excepting to sit down now and then for a few minutes by the wayside, I never paused in my flight the whole night through. Fatigue and want of food prevented me, it is true, from walking very fast; but the love of liberty was strong within me, and, by keeping steadily on, I succeeded in placing about eighteen miles between myself and Toulon. At five o'clock, just as the day began to dawn, I heard a peal of chimes, and found that I was approaching a large town. In order to avoid this town, I was forced to turn back for some distance, and take to the heights. The sun had now risen, and I dared go no farther; so, having pulled some turnips in a field as I went along, I took refuge in a little lonely copse in a hollow among the hills, and there lay all day in safety. When night again closed in, I resumed my journey, keeping always among the mountains, and coming now and then on grand glimpses of moonlit bays, and tranquil islands lying off the shore; now and then, on pastoral hamlets nestled up among the palmy heights; or on promontories overgrown with the cactus and the aloe. I rested all the second day in a ruined shed at the bottom of a deserted sand-pit, and, in the evening, feeling that I could no longer sustain life without some fitting nourishment, made my way down towards a tiny fishing village on the coast below. It was quite dark, by the time I reached the level ground. I walked boldly past the cottages of the fishermen, meeting only an old woman and a little child on the way, and knocked at the curé's door. He opened it himself. I told my story in half a dozen words. The good man believed and pitied me. He gave me food and wine, an old handkerchief to wrap about my head, an old coat to replace my convict's jacket, and two or three francs to help me on my way. I parted from him with tears.

I walked all that night again, and all the next, keeping somewhat close upon the coast, and hiding among the cliffs during the daytime. On the fifth morning, having left Antibes behind me during the night's march, I came to the banks of the Var; crossed the torrent about half a mile below the wooden bridge; plunged into the pine-woods on the Sardinian side of the frontier; and lay down to rest on Italian ground at last!

How, though comparatively safe, I still pursued my journey by the least frequented ways—how I bought a file at the first hamlet to which I came, and freed myself from the iron anklet—how, having lurked about Nice till my hair and beard had grown, I begged my way on to Genoa—how, at Genoa, I hung about the port, earning a scanty livelihood by any chance work that I could get, and so struggled, somehow, through the inclement winter—how, towards the early spring, I worked my passage on board a small trader from Genoa to Fiumicino, touching at all the ports along the coast—and how, coming slowly up the Tiber in a barge laden with oil and wine, I landed one evening in March on the Ripetta quay, in Rome; —how all these things happened, and what physical hardships I endured in the mean while, I have no time here to relate in detail. My object had been to get to Rome, and that object was at last attained. In so large a city, and at so great a distance from the scene of my imprisonment, I was personally safe. I might hope to turn my talents and education to account. I might even find friends among the strangers who would flock thither to the Easter festivals. Full of hope, therefore, I sought a humble lodging in the neighbourhood of the quay, gave up a day or two to the enjoyment of my liberty and of the sights of Rome, and then set myself to find some regular employment.

Regular employment, or, indeed, employment of any kind, was not, however, so easily to be obtained. It was a season of distress. The previous harvest had been a failure, and the winter unusually severe. There had also been disturbances in Naples, and the travellers this spring were fewer by some thousands than the ordinary average. So dull a carnival had not been known for years. The artists had sold no paintings, and the sculptors no statues. The cameo-cutters and mosaicists were starving. The tradesmen, the hotel-keepers, the professional ciceroni, were all complaining bitterly. Day by day, my hopes faded and my prospects darkened. Day by day, the few scudi I had scraped together on the passage melted away. I had thought to obtain a clerkship, or a secretaryship, or a situation in some public library. Before three weeks were over, I would gladly have swept a studio. At length there came a day when I saw nothing before me but starvation; what my last bajocco was expended; when my padrone (or landlord) shut the door in my face, and I knew not where to turn for a meal or a shelter. All that afternoon, I wandered hopeless about the streets. It was Good Friday, of all days in the year. The churches were hung with black; the bells were tolling; the thoroughfares were crowded with people in mourning. I went into the little church of Santa Martina. They were chanting a miserere, probably with no great skill, but with a pathos that seemed to open up all the sources of my despair.

Outcast that I was, I slept that night under a dark arch near the theatre of Marcellus. The morning dawned upon a glorious day, and I crept out, shivering, into the sunshine. Lying crouched against a bit of warm wall, I caught myself wondering more than once how long it would be worth while to endure the agonies of hunger, and whether the brown waters of the Tiber were deep enough to drown a man. It seemed hard to die so young. My future might have been so pleasant, so honourable. The rough life that I had been leading of late, too, had strengthened me in every way, physically and mentally. I had grown taller. My muscles were more developed. I was twice as active, as energetic, as resolute as I had been a year before. And of what use were these things to me? I must die, and they could only serve to make me die the harder.

I got up and wandered about the streets, as I had wandered the day before. Once I asked for alms, and was repulsed. I followed mechanically in the stream of carriages and foot passengers, and found myself, by-and-by, in the midst of the crowd that ebbs and flows continually about Saint Peter's during Easter week. Stupified and weary, I turned aside into the vestibule of the Sagrestia, and cowered down in the shelter of a doorway. Two gentlemen were reading a printed paper wafered against a pillar close by.

"Good Heavens!" said one to the other, " that a man should risk his neck for a few pauls!"

"Ay, and with the knowledge that out of eighty workmen, six or eight are dashed to pieces every time," added his companion.

"Shocking! Why, that is an average of ten per cent!"

"No less. It is a desperate service."

"But a fine sight," said the first speaker, philosophically; and with this they walked away.

I sprang to my feet, and read the placard with avidity It was headed "Illumination of Saint Peter's," and announced that, eighty workmen being required for the lighting of the dome and cupola, and three hundred for the cornices, pillars, colonnade, and so forth, the amministratore was empowered, &c. &c. In conclusion, it stated that every workman employed on the dome and cupola should receive in payment, a dinner and twenty-four pauls, the wages of the rest being less than a third of that sum.

A desperate service, it was true; but I was a desperate man. After all, I could but die, and I might as well die after a good dinner as from starvation. I went at once to the amministratore, was entered in his list, received a couple of pauls as earnest of the contract, and engaged to present myself punctually at eleven o'clock on the following morning. That evening I supped at a street stall, and, for a few bajocchi, obtained leave to sleep on some straw, in a loft over a stable at the back of the Via del Arco.

At eleven o'clock on the morning of Easter Sunday, April the sixteenth, I found myself, accordingly, in the midst of a crowd of poor fellows, most of whom, I dare say, were as wretched as myself, waiting at the door of the administrator's office. The piazza in front of the cathedral was like a moving mosaic of life and colour. The sun was shining, the fountains were playing, the flags were flying over Saint Angelo. It was a glorious sight; but I saw it for only a few moments. As the clocks struck the hour, the folding-doors were thrown open, and we passed, in a crowd, into a hall, where two long tables were laid for our accommodation. A couple of sentinels stood at the door; an usher marshalled us, standing, round the tables; and a priest read grace.

As he began to read, a strange sensation came upon me. I felt impelled to look across to the opposite table, and there . . . yes, by Heaven! there I saw Gasparo.

He was looking full at me, but his eyes dropped on meeting mine. I saw him turn lividly white. The recollection of all he had made me suffer, and of the dastardly blow that he had dealt me on the day of our flight, overpowered for the moment even my surprise at seeing him in this place. Oh that I might live to meet him yet, under the free sky, where no priest was praying, and no guards were by!

The grace was over, we sat down, and fell to. Not even anger had power to blunt the edge of my appetite just then. I ate like a famishing wolf, and so did most of the others. We were allowed no wine, and the doors were locked upon us, that we might not procure any elsewhere. It was a wise regulation, considering the task we had to perform; but it made us none the less noisy. Under certain circumstances, danger intoxicates like wine; and on this Easter Sunday, we eighty sanpietrini, any one of whom might have his brains dashed about the leads before supper-time, ate, talked, jested, and laughed, with a wild gaiety that had in it something appalling.

The dinner lasted long, and when no one seemed disposed to eat more, the tables were cleared. Most of the men threw themselves on the floor and benches, and went to sleep; Gasparo among the number. Seeing this, I could refrain no longer. I went over, and stirred him roughly with my foot.

"Gasparo! You know me?"

He looked up, sullenly.

"Devil's mass! I thought you were at Toulon."

"It is not your fault that I am not at Toulon! Listen to me. If you and I survive this night, you shall answer to me for your treachery!"

He glared at me from under his deep brows, and, without replying, turned over on his face again, as if to sleep.

"Ecco un maladetto!" (There's an accursed fellow!), said one of the others, with a significant shrug, as I came away.

"Do you know anything of him?" I asked, eagerly.

"Cospetto! I know nothing of him; but that solitude is said to have made him a Wolf."

I could learn no more, so I also stretched myself upon the floor, as far as possible from my enemy, and fell profoundly asleep.

At seven, the guards roused those who still slept, and served each man with a small mug of thin wine. We were then formed into a double file, marched round by the back of the cathedral, and conducted up an inclined plane to the roof below the dome. From this point, a long series of staircases and winding passages carried us up between the double walls of the dome; and, at different stages in the ascent, a certain number of us were detached and posted ready for work. I was detached about half way up, and I saw Gasparo going higher still. When we were all posted, the superintendents came round and gave us our instructions. At a given signal, every man was to pass out through the loophole or window before which he was placed, and seat himself astride upon a narrow shelf of wood hanging to a strong rope just below. This rope came through the window, was wound round a roller, and secured from within. At the next signal, a lighted torch would be put into his right hand, and he was to grasp the rope firmly with his left. At the third signal, the rope was to be unwound from within by an assistant placed there for the purpose, he was to be allowed to slide rapidly down, over the curve of the dome, and, while thus sliding, was to apply his torch to every lamp he passed in his downward progress.

Having received these instructions, we waited, each man at his window, until the first signal should be given.

It was fast getting dark, and the silver illumination had been lighted since seven. All the great ribs of the dome, as far as I could see: all the cornices and friezes of the façade below; all the columns and parapets of the great colonnade surrounding the piazza four hundred feet below, were traced out in lines of paper lanterns, the light from which, subdued by the paper, gleamed with a silvery fire which had a magical and wondrous look. Between and among these lanternoni, were placed, at different intervals all over the cathedral on the side facing the piazza, iron cups called padelle, ready filled with tallow and turpentine. To light those on the dome and cupola, was the perilous task of the sanpietrini; when they were all lighted, the golden illumination would be effected.

A few moments of intense suspense elapsed. At every second the evening grew darker, the lanternoni burned brighter, the surging hum of thousands in the piazza and streets below, rose louder to our ears. I felt the quickening breath of the assistant at my shoulder—I could almost hear the beating of my heart. Suddenly, like the passing of an electric current, the first signal flew from lip to lip. I got out, and crossed my legs firmly round the board—with the second signal, I seized the blazing torch—with the third, I felt myself launched, and, lighting every cup as I glided past, saw all the mountainous dome above and below me spring into lines of leaping flame. The clock was now striking eight, and when the last stroke sounded, the whole cathedral was glowing in outlines of fire. A roar, like the roar of a great ocean, rose up from the multitude below, and seemed to shake the very dome against which I was clinging. I could even see the light upon the gazing faces, the crowd upon the bridge of St. Angelo, and the boats swarming along the Tiber.

Having dropped safely to the full length of my rope, and lighted my allotted share of lamps, I was now sitting in secure enjoyment of this amazing scene. All at once, I felt the rope vibrate. I looked up, saw a man clinging by one hand to the iron rod supporting the padelle, and with the other . . . . Merciful Heaven! It was the Piedmontese firing the rope above me with his torch!

I had no time for thought—I acted upon instinct. It was done in one fearful moment. I clambered up like a cat, dashed my torch full in the solitary felon's face, and grasped the rope an inch or two above the spot where it was burning! Blinded and baffled, he uttered a terrible cry, and dropped like a stone. Through all the roar of the living ocean below, I could hear the dull crash with which he came down upon the leaded roof—resounding through all the years that have gone by since that night, I hear it now!

I had scarcely drawn breath, when I found myself being hauled up. The assistance came not a moment too soon, for I was sick and giddy with horror, and fainted as soon as I was safe in the corridor. The next day I waited on the amministratore, and told him all that had happened. My statement was corroborated by the vacant rope from which Gasparo had descended, and the burnt fragment by which I had been drawn up. The amministratore repeated my story to a prelate high in office; and while none, even of the sanpietrini, suspected that my enemy had come to his death in any unusual manner, the truth was whispered from palace to palace until it reached the Vatican. I received much sympathy, and such pecuniary assistance as enabled me to confront the future without fear. Since that time my fortunes have been various, and I have lived in many countries.

IV.

PICKING UP WAIFS AT SEA.

SOME little time elapsed, after the French gentleman's narrative was over, before any more visitors made their appearance. At last, there sauntered in slowly a light-haired melancholy man; very tall, very stout; miserably dressed in cast-off garments; carrying a carpenter's basket, and looking as if he never expected any such windfall of luck as the chance of using the tools inside it. Surveying Mr. Traveller with watery light-blue eyes, this dismal individual explained (in better language than might have been expected from his personal appearance) that he was in search of work; and that, finding none, he had come in to stare at Mr. Mopes for want of anything better to do. His name was Heavysides; his present address was the Peal of Bells down in the village; if Mr. Traveller had the means of putting a job in his hands, he would be thankful for the same; if not, he would ask leave to sit down and rest himself agreeably by looking at Mr. Mopes.

Leave being granted, he sat down, and stared to his heart's content. He was not astonished, as the artist had been; he was not complacently impenetrable to surprise, like the Frenchman—he was simply curious to know why the Hermit had shut himself up. "When he first skewered that blanket round him, what had he got to complain of?" asked Heavysides. "Whatever his grievance is, I could match it, I think."

"Could you?" said Mr. Traveller. "By all means let us hear it."

There has never yet been discovered a man with a grievance, who objected to mention it. The carpenter was no exception to this general human rule. He entered on his grievance, without a moment's hesitation, in these words:

I SHALL consider it in the light of a personal favour, at starting, if you will compose your spirits to hear a pathetic story, and if you will kindly picture me in your own mind as a baby five minutes old.

Do I understand you to say that I am too big and too heavy to be pictured in anybody's mind as a baby? Perhaps I may be—but don't mention my weight again, if you please. My weight has been the grand misfortune of my life. It spoilt all my prospects (as you will presently hear) before I was two days old.

My story begins thirty-one years ago, at eleven o'clock in the forenoon; and starts with the great mistake of my first appearance in this world, at sea, on board the merchant ship Adventure, Captain Gillop, five hundred tons burthen, coppered, and carrying an experienced surgeon.

In presenting myself to you (which I am now about to do) at that eventful period of my life, when I was from five to ten minutes old; and in withdrawing myself again from your notice (so as not to trouble you with more than a short story), before the time when I cut my first tooth, I need not hesitate to admit that I speak on hearsay knowledge only. It is knowledge, however, that may be relied on, for all that. My information comes from Captain Gillop, commander of The Adventure (who sent it to me in the form of a letter); from Mr. Jolly, experienced surgeon of The Adventure (who wrote it for me—most unfeelingly, as I think—in the form of a humorous narrative); and from Mrs. Drabble, stewardess of The Adventure (who told it me by word of mouth). Those three persons were, in various degrees, spectators—I may say, astonished spectators—of the events which I have now to relate.

The Adventure, at the time I speak of, was bound out from London to Australia. I suppose you know, without my telling you, that thirty years ago was long before the time of the gold-finding and the famous clipper ships. Building in the new colony, and sheep-farming far up inland, were the two main employments of those days; and the passengers on board our vessel were consequently builders or sheep-farmers, almost to a man.

A ship of five hundred tons, well loaded with cargo, doesn't offer first-rate accommodation to a large number of passengers. Not that the gentlefolks in the cabin had any great reason to complain. There, the passage-money, which was a good round sum, kept them what you call select. One or two berths, in this part of the ship, were even empty and going a begging, in consequence of there being only four cabin passengers. These are their names and descriptions:

Mr. Sims, a middle-aged man, going out on a building speculation. Mr. Purling, a weakly young gentleman, sent on a long sea-voyage for the benefit of his health. Mr. and Mrs. Smallchild, a young married couple with a little independence, which Mr. Smallchild proposed to make a large one by sheep-farming. This gentleman was reported to the captain, as being very good company when on shore. But the sea altered him to a certain extent. When Mr. Smallchild was not sick, he was eating and drinking; and when he was not eating and drinking, he was fast asleep

He was perfectly patient and good-humoured, and wonderfully nimble at running into his cabin when the qualms took him on a sudden—but, as for his being good company, nobody heard him say ten words together all through the voyage. And no wonder. A man can't talk in the qualms; a man can't talk while he is eating and drinking;· and a man can't talk when he is asleep. And that was Mr Smallchild's life. As for Mrs. Smallchild, she kept her cabin from first to last. But you will hear more of her presently.

These four cabin passengers, as I have already remarked, were well enough off for their accommodation. But the miserable people in the steerage—a poor place, at the best of times, on board The Adventurer—were all huddled together, men and women and children, higgledy-piggledy, like sheep in a pen; except that they hadn't got the same quantity of fine fresh air to blow over them. They were artisans and farm-labourers who couldn't make it out in the old country. I have no information either of their exact number or of their names. It doesn't matter: there was only one family among them which need be mentioned particularly—namely, the family of the Heavysides. To wit, Simon Heavysides, intelligent and well educated, a carpenter by trade; Martha Heavysides, his wife; and seven little Heavysides, their unfortunate offspring.—My father and mother and brothers and sisters, did I understand you to say? Don't be in a hurry; I recommend you to wait a little before you make quite sure of that circumstance.

Though I myself had not, perhaps—strictly speaking—come on board when the vessel left London, my ill-luck, as I firmly believe, had shipped in The Adventure to wait for me—and decided the nature of the voyage accordingly. Never was such a miserable time known. Stormy weather came down on us from all points of the compass, with intervals of light baffling winds, or dead calms. By the time The Adventure had been three months out, Captain Gillop's naturally sweet temper began to get soured. I leave you to say whether it was likely to be much improved by a piece of news which reached him from the region of the cabin, on the morning of the ninety-first day. It had fallen to a dead calm again; and the ship was rolling about helpless with her head all round the compass, when Mr. Jolly (from whose unfeeling narrative I repeat all conversations, exactly as they passed) came on deck to the captain, and addressed him in these words:

"I've got some news that will rather surprise you," said Mr. Jolly, smiling and rubbing his hands. (Although the experienced surgeon has not shown much sympathy for my troubles, I won't deny that his disposition was as good as his name. To this day, no amount of bad weather or hard work can upset Mr. Jolly's temper.)

"If it's news of a fair wind coming," grumbled the captain, "that would surprise me, on board this ship, I can promise you!"

"It's not exactly a wind coming," said Mr. Jolly. "It's another cabin passenger."

The captain looked round at the empty sea, with the land thousands of miles away, and with not a ship in sight—turned sharply on the experienced surgeon—eyed him hard—changed colour suddenly—and asked what he meant.

"I mean, there's a fifth cabin passenger coming on board," persisted Mr. Jolly, grinning from ear to ear—"introduced by Mrs. Smallchild—likely to join us, I should say, towards evening—size, nothing to speak of—sex, not known at present—manners and customs, probably squally."

"Do you really mean it?" asked the captain, backing away, and turning paler and paler.

"Yes; I do," answered Mr. Jolly, nodding hard at him.

"Then, I'll tell you what," cried Captain Gillop, suddenly flying into a violent passion. "I won't have it! The infernal weather has worried me out of my life and soul already—and I won't have it! Put it off, Jolly—tell her there isn't room enough for that sort of thing on board my vessel. What does she mean by taking us all in, in this way? Shameful! shameful!"

"No! no!" remonstrated Mr. Jolly. "Don't look at it in that light. It's her first child, poor thing. How should she know? Give her a little more experience, and I dare say——"

"Where's her husband?" broke in the captain, with a threatening look. "I'll speak my mind to him, at any rate."

Mr. Jolly consulted his watch before he answered.

"Half-past eleven," he said. "Let me consider a little. It's Mr. Smallchild's regular time just now for squaring accounts with the sea. He'll have done in a quarter of an hour. In five minutes more, he'll be fast asleep. At one o'clock, he'll eat a hearty lunch, and go to sleep again. At half-past two, he'll square accounts as before—and so on, till night. You'll make nothing of Mr. Smallchild, captain. Extraordinary man—wastes tissue, and repairs it again perpetually, in the most astonishing manner. If we are another month at sea, I believe we shall bring him into port totally comatose.—Hallo! What do you want?"

The steward's mate had approached the quarter-deck while the doctor was speaking. Was it a curious coincidence? This man also was grinning from ear to ear, exactly like Mr. Jolly.

"You're wanted in the steerage, sir," said the steward's mate to the doctor. "A woman taken bad, name of Heavysides."

"Nonsense!" cried Mr. Jolly. "Ha! ha! ha! You don't mean——Eh?"

"That's it, sir, sure enough," said the steward's mate, in the most positive manner.

Captain Gillop looked all round him, in silent desperation, lost his sea-legs for the first time these twenty years, staggered back till he was brought up all standing by the side of his own vessel, dashed his fist on the bulwark, and found language to express himself in, at the same moment.

"This ship is bewitched," said the captain, wildly. "Stop!" he called out, recovering himself a little, as the doctor bustled away to the steerage. "Stop! If it's true, Jolly, send her husband here aft to me. Damme, I'll have it out with one of the husbands!" said the captain, shaking his fist viciously at the empty air.

Ten minutes passed; and then, there came

staggering towards the captain, tottering this way and that with the rolling of the becalmed vessel, a long, lean, melancholy, light-haired man, with a Roman nose, a watery blue eye, and a complexion profusely spotted with large brown freckles. This was Simon Heavysides, the intelligent carpenter, with the wife and the family of seven small children on board.

"Oh! you're the man, are you?" said the captain.

The ship lurched heavily; and Simon Heavysides staggered away with a run to the opposite side of the deck, as if he preferred going straight overboard into the sea, to answering the captain's question.

"You're the man—are you?" repeated the captain, following him, seizing him by the collar, and pinning him up fiercely against the bulwark. "It's your wife—is it! You infernal rascal! what do you mean by turning my ship into a Lying-In Hospital? You have committed an act of mutiny; or, if it isn't mutiny, it's next door to it. I've put a man in irons for less! I've more than half a mind to put *you* in irons! Hold up, you slippery 'lubber! What do you mean by bringing passengers I don't bargain for on board my vessel? What have you got to say for yourself, before I clap the irons on you?"

"Nothing, sir," answered Simon Heavysides, with the meekest connubial resignation in his looks and manners. "As for the punishment you mentioned just now, sir," continued Simon, "I wish to say—having seven children more than I know how to provide for, and an eighth coming to make things worse—I respectfully wish to say, sir, that my mind is in irons already; and I don't know as it will make much difference if you put my body in irons along with it."

The captain mechanically let go of the carpenter's collar: the mild despair of the man melted him in spite of himself.

"Why did you come to sea? Why didn't you wait ashore till it was all over?" asked the captain, as sternly as he could.

"It's no use waiting, sir," remarked Simon. "In our line of life as soon as it's over, it begins again. There's no end to it that I can see," said the miserable carpenter, after a moment's meek consideration—"except the grave."

"Who's talking about the grave?" cried Mr. Jolly, coming up at that moment. "It's births we've got to do with on board this vessel—not burials. Captain Gillop, this woman, Martha Heavysides, can't be left in your crowded steerage, in her present condition. She must be moved off into one of the empty berths—and the sooner the better, I can tell you!"

The captain began to look savage again. A steerage passenger in one of his "state-rooms" was a nautical anomaly subversive of all discipline. He eyed the carpenter once more, as if he was mentally measuring him for a set of irons.

"I'm very sorry, sir," Simon remarked, politely —"very sorry that any inadvertence of mine or Mrs. Heavyside's——"

"Take your long carcase and your long tongue forward!" thundered the captain. "When talking will mend matters, I'll send for you again. Give your own orders, Jolly," he went on, re-

signedly, as Simon staggered off. "Turn the ship into a nursery as soon as you like!"

Five minutes later—so expeditious was Mr. Jolly—Martha Heavysides appeared horizontally on deck, shrouded in blankets, and supported by three men. When this interesting procession passed the captain, he shrank aside from it with as vivid an appearance of horror as if a wild bull was being carried by him instead of a British matron. The sleeping berths below opened on either side out of the main cabin. On the left-hand side (looking towards the ship's bowsprit) was Mrs. Smallchild. On the right hand side, opposite to her, the doctor established Mrs. Heavysides. A partition of canvas was next run up, entirely across the main cabin. The smaller of the two temporary rooms thus made, lay nearest the stairs leading on deck, and was left free to the public The larger was kept sacred to the doctor and his mysteries. When an old clothesbasket, emptied, cleaned, and comfortably lined with blankets (to serve for a make-shift cradle), had been, in due course of time, carried into the inner cabin, and had been placed midway between the two sleeping-berths, so as to be easily producible when wanted, the outward and visible preparations of Mr. Jolly were complete; the male passengers had all taken refuge on deck; and the doctor and stewardess were left in undisturbed possession of the lower regions.

While it was still early in the afternoon, the weather changed for the better. For once in a way, the wind came from the fair quarter; and The Adventurer bowled along pleasantly before it almost on an even keel. Captain Gillop mixed with the little group of male passengers on the quarter-deck, restored to his sweetest temper; and set them his customary example, after dinner, of smoking a cigar.

"If this fine weather lasts, gentlemen," he said, "we shall make out very well with our meals up here; and we shall have our two small extra cabin passengers christened on dry land in a week's time, if their mothers approve of it. How do you feel in your mind, sir, about your lady?"

Mr. Smallchild (to whom the inquiry was addressed) had his points of external personal resemblance to Simon Heavysides. He was neither so tall, nor so lean certainly—but he, too, had a Roman nose, and light hair, and watery blue eyes. With careful reference to his peculiar habits at sea, he had been placed conveniently close to the bulwark, and had been raised on a heap of old sails and cushions, so that he could easily get his head over the ship's side when occasion required. The food and drink which assisted in "restoring his tissue," when he was not asleep and not "squaring accounts with the sea," lay close to his hand. It was then a little after three o'clock; and the snore with which Mr. Smallchild answered the captain's inquiry showed that he had got round again, with the regularity of clockwork, to the period of the day when he recruited himself with sleep.

"What an insensible blockhead that man is!" said Mr. Sims, the middle-aged passenger; looking across the deck contemptuously at Mr. Smallchild.

"If the sea had the same effect on you that it

has on him," retorted the invalid passenger, Mr. Purling, "you would be just as insensible yourself."

Mr. Purling (who was a man of sentiment) disagreed with Mr. Sims (who was a man of business), on every conceivable subject, all through the voyage. Before, however, they could continue the dispute about Mr. Smallchild, the doctor surprised them by appearing from the cabin.

"Any news below, Jolly?" asked the captain, anxiously.

"None whatever," answered the doctor. "I've come to idle the afternoon away up here, along with the rest of you."

As events turned out, Mr. Jolly idled away an hour and a half exactly. At the end of that time, Mrs. Drabble the stewardess appeared with a face of mystery, and whispered nervously to the doctor:

"Please to step below directly, sir."

"Which of them is it?" asked Mr. Jolly.

"*Both* of them," answered Mrs. Drabble, emphatically.

The doctor looked grave; the stewardess looked frightened. The two immediately disappeared together.

"I suppose, gentlemen," said Captain Gillop, addressing Mr. Purling, Mr. Sims, and the first mate, who had just joined the party, "I suppose it's only fit and proper, in the turn things have taken, to shake up Mr. Smallchild? And I don't doubt but what we ought to have the other husband handy, as a sort of polite attention under the circumstances. Pass the word forward, there, for Simon Heavysides. Mr. Smallchild, sir! rouse up! Here's your good lady——Hang me, gentlemen, if I know exactly how to put it to him."

"Yes. Thank you," said Mr. Smallchild, opening his eyes drowsily. "Biscuit and cold bacon, as usual—when I'm ready. I'm not ready yet. Thank you. Good afternoon." Mr. Smallchild closed his eyes again, and became, in the doctor's phrase, "totally comatose."

Before Captain Gillop could hit on any new plan for rousing this imperturbable passenger, Simon Heavysides once more approached the quarter-deck.

"I spoke a little sharp to you, just now, my man," said the captain, "being worried in my mind by what's going on on board this vessel. But I'll make it up to you, never fear. Here's your wife in, what they call, an interesting situation. It's only right you should be within easy hail of her. I look upon you, Heavysides, as a steerage-passenger in difficulties; and I freely give you leave to stop here along with us till it's all over."

"You are very good, sir," said Simon: "and I am indeed thankful to you and to these gentlemen. But, please to remember, I have seven children already in the steerage—and there's nobody left to mind 'em but me. My wife has got over it uncommonly well, sir, on seven previous occasions—and I don't doubt but what she'll conduct herself in a similar manner on the eighth. It will be a satisfaction to her mind, Captain Gillop and gentlemen, if she knows I'm out of the way, and minding the children. For which reason, I

respectfully take my leave." With those words, Simon made his bow, and returned to his family.

"Well, gentlemen, these two husbands take it easy enough, at any rate!" said the captain. "One of them is used to it, to be sure; and the other is——"

Here a banging of cabin doors below, and a hurrying of footsteps, startled the speaker and his audience into momentary silence and attention.

"Ease her with the helm, Williamson!" said Captain Gillop, addressing the man who was steering the vessel. "In my opinion, gentlemen, the less the ship pitches the better, in the turn things are taking now."

The afternoon wore on into evening, and evening into night. Mr. Smallchild performed the daily ceremonies of his nautical existence as punctually as usual. He was aroused to a sense of Mrs. Smallchild's situation when he took his biscuit and bacon; lost the sense again when the time came round for "squaring his accounts;" recovered it in the interval which ensued before he went to sleep; lost it again, as a matter of course, when his eyes closed once more—and so on through the evening and early night. Simon Heavysides received messages occasionally (through the captain's care), teling him to keep his mind easy; returned messages mentioning that his mind was easy, and that the children were pretty quiet, but never approached the deck in his own person. Mr. Jolly now and then showed himself—said "All right,—no news," took a little light refreshment, and disappeared again, as cheerful as ever. The fair breeze still held; the captain's temper remained unruffled; the man at the helm eased the vessel, from time to time, with the most anxious consideration. Ten o'clock came: the moon rose and shone superbly; the nightly grog made its appearance on the quarter-deck; the captain gave the passengers the benefit of his company; and still nothing happened. Twenty minutes more of suspense slowly succeeded each other—and then, at last, Mr. Jolly was seen suddenly to ascend the cabin stairs.

To the amazement of the little group on the quarter-deck, the doctor held Mrs. Drabble, the stewardess, fast by the arm, and, without taking the slightest notice of the captain or the passengers, placed her on the nearest seat he could find. As he did this, his face became visible in the moonlight, and displayed to the startled spectators an expression of blank consternation.

"Compose yourself, Mrs. Drabble," said the doctor, in tones of unmistakable alarm. "Keep quiet, and let the air blow over you. Collect yourself, ma'am—for Heaven's sake, collect yourself!"

Mrs. Drabble made no answer. She beat her hands vacantly on her knees, and stared straight before her, like a woman panic-stricken.

"What's wrong?" asked the captain, setting down his glass of grog in dismay. "Anything amiss with those two unfortunate women?"

"Nothing," said the doctor. "Both doing admirably well."

"Anything queer with their babies?" continued the captain. "Are there more than you bargained for, Jolly? Twins, for instance?"

"No! no!" replied Mr. Jolly, impatiently. "A baby apiece—both boys—both in first rate condition. Judge for yourselves," added the doctor, as the two new cabin-passengers tried their lungs, below, for the first time, and found that they answered their purpose in the most satisfactory manner.

"What the devil's amiss, then, with you and Mrs. Drabble?" persisted the captain, beginning to lose his temper again.

"Mrs. Drabble and I are two innocent people, and we have got into the most dreadful scrape that you ever heard of!" was Mr. Jolly's startling answer.

The captain, followed by Mr. Purling and Mr. Sims, approached the doctor with looks of horror. Even the man at the wheel stretched himself over it as far as he could to hear what was coming next. The only uninterested person was Mr. Smallchild. His time had come round for going to sleep again, and he was snoring peacefully, with his biscuit and bacon close beside him.

"Let's hear the worst of it at once, Jolly," said the captain, a little impatiently.

The doctor paid no heed to this request. His whole attention was absorbed by Mrs. Drabble. "Are you better now, ma'am?" he asked, anxiously.

"No better in my mind," answered Mrs. Drabble, beginning to beat her knees again. "Worse, if anything."

"Listen to me," said Mr. Jolly, coaxingly. "I'll put the whole case over again to you, in a few plain questions You'll find it all come back to your memory, if you only follow me attentively, and if you take time to think and collect yourself before you attempt to answer."

Mrs. Drabble bowed her head in speechless submission—and listened. Everybody else on the quarter-deck listened, except the impenetrable Mr. Smallchild.

"Now, ma'am!" said the doctor. "Our troubles began in Mrs. Heavysides' cabin, which is situated on the starboard side of the ship?"

"They did, sir," replied Mrs. Drabble.

"Good! We went backwards and forwards, an infinite number of times, between Mrs. Heavysides (starboard) and Mrs. Smallchild (larboard)—but we found that Mrs. Heavysides, having got the start, kept it—and when I called out, 'Mrs. Drabble! here's a chopping boy for you: come and take him!'—I called out starboard, didn't I?"

"Starboard, sir—I'll take my oath of it," said Mrs. Drabble.

"Good, again! 'Here is a chopping boy,' I said. 'Take him, ma'am, and make him comfortable in the cradle.' And you took him, and made him comfortable in the cradle, accordingly? Now, where was the cradle?"

"In the main cabin, sir," replied Mrs. Drabble.

"Just so! In the main cabin, because we hadn't got room for it in either of the sleeping-cabins You put the starboard baby (otherwise Heavysides) in the clothes-basket cradle in the main cabin. Good, once more. How was the cradle placed?"

"Crosswise to the ship, sir," said Mrs. Drabble.

"Crosswise to the ship? That is to say, with one side longwise towards the stern of the vessel, and one side longwise towards the bows. Bear that in mind—and now follow me a little farther. No! no! don't say you can't, and your head's in a whirl. My next question will steady it. Carry your mind on half an hour, Mrs. Drabble. At the end of half an hour, you heard my voice again; and my voice called out—'Mrs. Drabble! here's another chopping boy for you: come and take him!'—and you came and took him larboard, didn't you?"

"Larboard, sir, I don't deny it," answered Mrs. Drabble.

"Better and better! 'Here is another chopping boy,' I said. 'Take him, ma'am, and make him comfortable in the cradle, along with number one.' And you took the larboard baby (otherwise Smallchild) and made him comfortable in the cradle along with the starboard baby (otherwise Heavysides), accordingly? Now, what happened after that?"

"Don't ask me, sir!" exclaimed Mrs. Drabble, losing her self-control, and wringing her hands desperately.

"Steady, ma'am! I'll put it to you as plain as print. Steady! and listen to me. Just as you had made the larboard baby comfortable, I had occasion to send you into the starboard (or Heavysides) cabin, to fetch something which I wanted in the larboard (or Smallchild) cabin; I kept you there a little while along with me; I left you, and went into the Heavysides cabin, and called to you to bring me something I wanted out of the Smallchild cabin, but before you got half way across the main cabin, I said 'No; stop where you are, and I'll come to you;' immediately after which, Mrs. Smallchild alarmed you, and you came across to me of your own accord; and, thereupon, I stopped you in the main cabin, and said, 'Mrs. Drabble, your mind's getting confused, sit down and collect your scattered intellects; and you sat down, and tried to collect them——?"

("And couldn't, sir," interposed Mrs. Drabble, parenthetically. "Oh, my head! my head!")

—"And tried to collect your scattered intellects, and couldn't?" continued the doctor. "And the consequence was, when I came out from the Smallchild cabin to see how you were getting on, I found you with the clothes-basket cradle hoisted up on the cabin table, staring down at the babies inside with your mouth dropped open, and both your hands twisted in your hair? And when I said, 'Anything wrong with either of those fine boys, Mrs. Drabble?' you caught me by the coat-collar, and whispered in my right ear these words: 'Lord save us and help us, Mr. Jolly, I've confused the two babies in my mind, and I don't know which is which!'"

"And I don't know now!" cried Mrs. Drabble, hysterically. "Oh, my head! my head! I don't know now!"

"Captain Gillop and gentlemen," said Mr. Jolly, wheeling round and addressing his audience with the composure of sheer despair, "that is the Scrape—and, if you ever heard of a worse one, I'll trouble you to compose this miserable woman by mentioning it immediately."

Captain Gillop looked at Mr. Purling and Mr.

Sims. Mr. Purling and Mr. Sims looked at Captain Gillop. They were all three thunderstruck—and no wonder.

"Can't *you* throw any light on it, Jolly?" inquired the captain, who was the first to recover himself.

"If you knew what I have had to do below, you wouldn't ask me such a question as that," replied the doctor. "Remember that I have had the lives of two women and two children to answer for—remember that I have been cramped up in two small sleeping-cabins, with hardly room to turn round in, and just light enough from two miserable little lamps to see my hand before me—remember the professional difficulties of the situation, the ship rolling about under me all the while, and the stewardess to compose into the bargain ;—bear all that in mind, will you, and then tell me how much spare time I had on my hands for comparing two boys together inch by inch—two boys born at night, within half an hour of each other, on board a ship at sea. Ha! ha! I only wonder the mothers and the boys and the doctor are all five of them alive to tell the story!"

"No marks on one or other of them, that happened to catch your eye?" asked Mr. Sims.

"They must have been strongish marks to catch my eye in the light I had to work by, and in the professional difficulties I had to grapple with," said the doctor. "I saw they were both straight, well-formed children—and that's all I saw."

"Are their infant features sufficiently developed to indicate a family likeness?" inquired Mr. Purling. "Should you say they took after their fathers or their mothers?"

"Both of them have light eyes, and light hair—such as it is," replied Mr. Jolly, doggedly. "Judge for yourself."

"Mr. Smallchild has light eyes and light hair," remarked Mr. Sims.

"And Simon Heavysides has light eyes and light hair," rejoined Mr. Purling.

"I should recommend waking Mr. Smallchild, and sending for Mr. Heavysides, and letting the two fathers toss up for it," suggested Mr. Sims.

"The parental feeling is not to be trifled with in that heartless manner," retorted Mr. Purling. "I should recommend trying the Voice of Nature."

"What may that be, sir?" inquired Captain Gillop, with great curiosity.

"The maternal instinct," replied Mr. Purling. "The mother's intuitive knowledge of her own child."

"Ay, ay!" said the captain. "Well thought of. What do you say, Jolly, to the Voice of Nature?"

The doctor held up his hand impatiently. He was engaged in resuming the effort to rouse Mrs. Drabble's memory by a system of amateur cross-examination, with the unsatisfactory result of confusing her more hopelessly than ever. Could she put the cradle back, in her own mind, into its original position? No. Could she remember whether she laid the starboard baby (otherwise Heavysides) on the side of the cradle nearest the stern of the ship, or nearest the bows?

No. Could she remember any better about the larboard baby (otherwise Smallchild)? No. Why did she move the cradle on to the cabin table, and so bewilder herself additionally, when she was puzzled already? Because it came over her, on a sudden, that she had forgotten, in the dreadful confusion of the time, which was which; and of course she wanted to look closer at them, and see; and she couldn't see; and to her dying day she could never forgive herself; and let them throw her overboard, for a miserable wretch, if they liked,—and so on, till the persevering doctor was wearied out at last, and gave up Mrs. Drabble, and gave up with her, the whole case.

"I see nothing for it but the Voice of Nature," said the captain, holding fast to Mr. Purling's idea. "Try it, Jolly—you can but try it."

"Something must be done," said the doctor. "I can't leave the women alone any longer; and the moment I get below they will both ask for their babies. Wait here, till you're fit to be seen, Mrs. Drabble, and then follow me. Voice of Nature!" added Mr. Jolly, contemptuously, as he descended the cabin stairs. "Oh yes, I'll try it—much good the Voice of Nature will do us, gentlemen. You shall judge for yourselves."

Favoured by the night, Mr. Jolly cunningly turned down the dim lamps in the sleeping cabins to a mere glimmer, on the pretext that light was bad for his patients' eyes. He then took up the first of the two unlucky babies that came to hand, marked the clothes in which it was wrapped with a blot of ink, and carried it in to Mrs. Smallchild. choosing her cabin merely because he happened to be nearest to it. The second baby (distinguished by having no mark) was taken by Mrs. Drabble to Mrs. Heavysides. For a certain time, the two mothers and the two babies were left together. They were then separated again by medical order; and were afterwards reunited, with the difference that the marked baby went on this occasion to Mrs. Heavysides, and the unmarked baby to Mrs. Smallchild—the result, in the obscurity of the sleeping cabins, proving to be that one baby did just as well as the other, and that the Voice of Nature was (as Mr. Jolly had predicted) totally incompetent to settle the existing difficulty.

"While night serves us, Captain Gillop, we shall do very well," said the doctor, after he had duly reported the failure of Mr. Purling's suggested experiment. "But when morning comes, and daylight shows the difference between the children, we must be prepared with a course of some kind. If the two mothers, below, get the slightest suspicion of the case as it really stands, the nervous shock of the discovery may do dreadful mischief. They must be kept deceived, till they're up and well again, in the interests of their own health. We must choose a baby for each of them when to-morrow comes, and then hold to the choice, till the mothers are up again. The question is, who's to take the responsibility. I don't usually stick at trifles—but I candidly admit that *I'm* afraid of it."

"I decline meddling in the matter, on the ground that I am a perfect stranger," said Mr. Sims.

"And I object to interfere, from precisely similar motives," added Mr. Purling; agreeing for the first time with a proposition that emanated from his natural enemy all through the voyage.

"Wait a minute, gentlemen," said Captain Gillop, "I've got this difficult matter, as I think, in its right bearings. We must make a clean breast of it to the husbands, and let them take the responsibility."

"I believe they won't accept it," observed Mr. Sims.

"And I believe they will," asserted Mr. Purling, relapsing into his old habits.

"If they won't," said the captain, firmly, "I'm master on board this ship—and, as sure as my name's Thomas Gillop, I'll take the responsibility!"

This courageous declaration settled all difficulties for the time being; and a council was held to decide on future proceedings. It was resolved to remain passive until the next morning, on the last faint chance that a few hours' sleep might compose Mrs. Drabble's bewildered memory. The babies were to be moved into the main cabin before the daylight grew bright —or, in other words, before Mrs. Smallchild or Mrs. Heavysides could identify the infant who had passed the night with her for the time being. The doctor and the captain were to be assisted by Mr. Purling, Mr. Sims, and the first mate, in the capacity of witnesses; and the assembly so constituted was to meet, in consideration of the emergency of the case, at six o'clock in the morning, punctually.

At six o'clock accordingly, with the weather fine, and the wind still fair, the proceedings began. For the last time Mr. Jolly cross-examined Mrs. Drabble, assisted by the captain, and supervised by the witnesses. Nothing whatever was elicited from the unfortunate stewardess. The doctor pronounced her confusion to be chronic, and the captain and the witnesses unanimously agreed with him.

The next experiment tried was the revelation of the true state of the case to the husbands. Mr. Smallchild happened, on this occasion, to be "squaring his accounts" for the morning; and the first articulate words which escaped him in reply to the disclosure, were: "Devilled biscuit and anchovy paste." Further perseverance merely elicited an impatient request that they would "pitch him overboard at once, and the two babies along with him" Serious remonstrance was tried next, with no better effect. "Settle it how you like," said Mr. Smallchild, faintly. "Do you leave it to me, sir, as commander of this vessel?" asked Captain Gillop. (No answer.) "Nod your head, sir, if you can't speak." Mr. Smallchild nodded his head round-wise on his pillow—and fell asleep. "Does that count for leave to me to act?" asked Captain Gillop of the witnesses. And the witnesses answered, decidedly, Yes.

The ceremony was then repeated with Simon Heavysides, who responded, as became so intelligent a man, with a proposal of his own for solving the difficulty.

"Captain Gillop and gentlemen," said the carpenter, with fluent and melancholy politeness, "I should wish to consider Mr Smallchild before myself in this matter. I am quite willing to part with my baby (whichever he is); and I respectfully propose that Mr. Smallchild should take both the children, and so make quite sure that he has really got possession of his own son."

The only immediate objection to this ingenious proposition was started by the doctor; who sarcastically inquired of Simon "what he thought Mrs. Heavysides would say to it?" The carpenter confessed that this consideration had escaped him; and that Mrs. Heavysides was only too likely to be an irremovable obstacle in the way of the proposed arrangement. The witnesses, all thought so too; and Heavysides and his idea were dismissed together, after Simon had first gratefully expressed his entire readiness to leave it all to the captain.

"Very well, gentlemen," said Captain Gillop. "As commander on board, I reckon next after the husbands in the matter of responsibility— I've considered this difficulty in all its bearings —and I'm prepared to deal with it. The Voice of Nature (which you proposed, Mr. Purling) has been found to fail. The tossing up for it (which you proposed, Mr. Sims) doesn't square altogether with my notions of what's right in a very serious business. No, sir! I've got my own plan; and I'm now about to try it. Follow me below, gentlemen, to the steward's pantry."

The witnesses looked round on one another in the profoundest astonishment—and followed.

"Saunders," said the captain, addressing the steward. "Bring out the scales."

The scales were of the ordinary kitchen sort, with a tin tray, on one side, to hold the commodity to be weighed, and a stout iron slab on the other to support the weights. Saunders placed these scales upon a neat little pantry table, fitted on the ball-and-socket principle, so as to save the breaking of crockery by swinging with the motion of the ship.

"Put a clean duster in the tray," said the captain. "Doctor," he continued, when this had been done, "shut the doors of the sleeping-berths (for fear of the women hearing anything); and oblige me by bringing those two babies in here."

"Oh, sir!" exclaimed Mrs. Drabble, who had been peeping guiltily at the proceedings—"oh, don't hurt the little dears! If anybody suffers, let it be me!"

"Hold your tongue, if you please, ma'am," said the captain. "And keep the secret of these proceedings, if you wish to keep your place. If the ladies ask for their children, say they will have them in ten minutes' time."

The doctor came in, and set down the clothes-basket cradle on the pantry floor. Captain Gillop immediately put on his spectacles, and closely examined the two unconscious innocents who lay beneath him.

"Six of one and half a dozen of the other,"

said the captain. "I don't see any difference between them. Wait a bit, though! Yes, I do. One's a bald baby. Very good. We'll begin with that one. Doctor, strip the bald baby, and put him in the scales"

The bald baby protested—in his own language —but in vain. In two minutes he was flat on his back in the tin tray, with the clean duster under him to take the chill off.

"Weigh him accurately, Saunders," continued the captain. "Weigh him, if necessary, to an eighth of an ounce. Gentlemen! watch this proceeding closely; it's a very important one."

While the steward was weighing and the witnesses were watching, Captain Gillop asked his first mate for the log-book of the ship, and for pen and ink.

"How much, Saunders?" asked the captain, opening the book.

"Seven pounds, one ounce, and a quarter," answered the steward.

"Right, gentlemen?" pursued the captain.

"Quite right," said the witnesses.

"Bald child—distinguished as Number One —weight, seven pounds, one ounce, and a quarter (avoirdupois)," repeated the captain, writing down the entry in his log-book. "Very good. We'll put the bald baby back now, doctor; and try the hairy one next."

The hairy one protested—also in his own language—and also in vain.

"How much, Saunders!" asked the captain.

"Six pounds, fourteen ounces, and three-quarters," replied the steward.

"Right, gentlemen?" inquired the captain.

"Quite right," answered the witnesses.

"Hairy child—distinguished as Number Two, weight six pounds, fourteen ounces, and three-quarters (avoirdupois)," repeated, and wrote, the captain. "Much obliged to you, Jolly—that will do. When you have got the other baby back in the cradle, tell Mrs. Drabble neither of them must be taken out of it, till further orders; and them be so good as to join me and these gentlemen on deck. If anything of a discussion rises up among us, we won't run the risk of being heard in the sleeping-berths." With these words Captain Gillop led the way on deck, and the first mate followed with the log-book and the pen and ink.

"Now, gentlemen," began the captain, when the doctor had joined the assembly, "my first mate will open these proceedings by reading from the log a statement which I have written myself, respecting this business, from beginning to end. If you find it all equally correct with the statement of what the two children weigh, I'll trouble you to sign it, in your quality of witnesses, on the spot."

The first mate read the narrative, and the witnesses signed it, as perfectly correct. Captain Gillop then cleared his throat, and addressed his expectant audience in these words:

"You'll all agree with me, gentlemen, that justice is justice; and that like must to like. Here's my ship of five hundred tons, fitted with her spars accordingly. Say, she's a schooner of a hundred and fifty tons, the veriest landsman among you, in that case, wouldn't put such

masts as these into her. Say, on the other hand, she's an Indiaman of a thousand tons, would our spars (excellent good sticks as they are, gentlemen) be suitable for a vessel of that capacity? Certainly not. A schooner's spars to a schooner, and a ship's spars to a ship, in fit and fair proportion. In this serious difficulty, I take my stand on that principle. And my decision is: give the heaviest of the two babies to the heaviest of the two women; and let the lightest then fall, as a matter of course, to the other. In a week's time, if this weather holds, we shall all (please God) be in port; and if there's a better way out of this mess than my way, the parsons and lawyers ashore may find it, and welcome."

With those words the captain closed his oration; and the assembled council immediately sanctioned the proposal submitted to them, with all the unanimity of men who had no idea of their own to set up in opposition. Mr. Jolly was next requested (as the only available authority) to settle the question of weight between Mrs. Smallchild and Mrs. Heavysides, and decided it, without a moment's hesitation, in favour of the carpenter's wife, on the indisputable ground that she was the tallest and the stoutest woman of the two. Thereupon, the bald baby, "distinguished as Number One," was taken into Mrs. Heavysides' cabin; and the hairy baby, "distinguished as Number Two," was accorded to Mrs. Smallchild; the Voice of Nature, neither in the one case nor in the other, raising the slightest objection to the captain's principle of distribution. Before seven o'clock, Mr. Jolly reported that the mothers and sons, larboard and starboard, were as happy and comfortable as any four people on board ship could possibly wish to be; and the captain thereupon dismissed the council with these parting words:

"We'll get the studding-sails on the ship now, gentlemen, and make the best of our way to port. Breakfast, Saunders, in half an hour, and plenty of it! I doubt if that unfortunate Mrs. Drabble has heard the last of this business yet. We must all lend a hand, gentlemen, and pull her through if we can. In other respects, the job's over, so far as we are concerned; and the parsons and the lawyers must settle it ashore."

But, the parsons and the lawyers did nothing of the sort, for the plain reason that nothing was to be done. In ten days the ship was in port, and the news was broken to the two mothers. Each one of the two adored her baby, after ten days' experience of it—and each one of the two was in Mrs. Drabble's condition of not knowing which was which. Every test was tried. First, the test by the doctor, who only repeated what he had told the captain. Secondly, the test by personal resemblance; which failed in consequence of the light hair, blue eyes, and Roman noses, shared in common by the fathers, and the light hair, blue eyes, and no noses worth mentioning, shared in common by the children. Thirdly, the test of Mrs. Drabble, which began and ended in fierce talking on one side and floods of tears on the other. Fourthly, the test by legal decision, which broke down through the total absence of any instructions for the law to act on. Fifthly, and lastly, the test by appeal to the husbands, which fell to the ground in consequence of the husbands knowing nothing about the matter in hand. The captain's barbarous test by weight, remained the test still—and here am I, a man of the lower order, without a penny to bless myself with, in consequence.

Yes! I was the bald baby of that memorable period. My excess in weight settled my destiny in life. The fathers and mothers on either side kept the babies according to the captain's principle of distribution, in despair of knowing what else to do. Mr. Smallchild—who was sharp enough, when not sea-sick—made his fortune. Simon Heavysides persisted in increasing his family, and died in the workhouse. Judge for yourself (as Mr. Jolly might say) how the two boys born at sea have fared in after-life. I, the bald baby, have seen nothing of the hairy baby for years past. He may be short, like Mr. Smallchild—but I happen to know that he is wonderfully like Heavysides, deceased, in the face. I may be tall like the carpenter—but I have the Smallchild eyes, hair, and expression, notwithstanding. Make what you can of that! You will find it come in the end to the same thing. Smallchild, junior, prospers in the world, because he weighed six pounds, fourteen ounces, and three-quarters. Heavysides, junior, fails in the world, because he weighed seven pounds, one ounce, and a quarter. There is the end of it, anyhow; and, if Mr. Hermit's outer crust will only let him, I recommend him to blush for his own grievance, whatever it is. As for Mr. Traveller, if he happens to have any loose silver about him, I'm not above taking it—and so I leave you, gentlemen, to settle the argument between you.

------◆------

V.

PICKING UP A POCKET-BOOK.

SEVERAL people came in at the gate, not only when the last speaker had withdrawn, but at various times throughout the day, from whom nothing could be extracted by the utmost ingenuity of Mr. Traveller, save what their calling was (when they had any), whence they came, and whither they were going. But, as those who had nothing to tell, clearly could tell nothing in justification of Mr. Mopes the Hermit, Mr. Traveller was almost as well satisfied with them as with any of the rest. Some of the many visitors came of a set purpose, attracted by curiosity; some, by chance, looking in to explore so desolate a place; many had often been there before, and came for drink and halfpence. These regular clients were all of the professed vagrant order: "and, as I observed to you," Mr. Traveller invariably remarked with coolness when they were gone, "are part of the Nuisance."

When any one approached, either purposely or accidentally, to whom the figure in the blanket was new, Mr. Traveller, acting as a self-constituted showman, did the honours of the place: referring to the Hermit as "our friend in there," and asking the visitor, without further explanation—lest his own impartiality should be called in question, if he could favour our friend in there with any little experience of the living and moving world? It was in answer to this inquiry, that a sunburnt gentleman of middle age, with fine bright eyes, and a remarkable air of determination and self-possession (he had come over from the assize-town, he said, to see the sight in the soot and cinders), spake thus:

OFFICE-HOURS were over, and we were all taking down our straw-hats from the pegs on which they dangled; ledgers were clasped, papers put away, desks locked, and the work of the day was at an end, when the white-haired cashier came sidling towards me. "Mr. Walford, sir, would you stay a moment? Would you step this way? The firm wish to speak to you?"

Good old Job Wiginton always described his employers, collectively, as "the firm." They were sacred beings in his eyes, were Spalding and Hausermann, and he had served them for a quarter of a century, with exemplary fidelity and respect. Job Wiginton, like myself, and like the senior partner in that great mercantile house, was an Englishman born and bred. He had kept the books of Spalding and Hausermann for twenty years at Philadelphia, and had cheerfully followed them to California, when they decided on settling in San Francisco City, five years before. The younger clerks, French or American for the most part, were rather disposed to make a butt of the simple honest old cashier, but he and I had been very good friends during the four years of my employment, and I always entertained a sincere respect for the old man's sterling good qualities. Now, however, for a reason I will presently explain, I was considerably taken aback by the communication which Mr. Wiginton made in his own formal way.

"The firm wish to see me?" I stammered, with a tell-tale colour rising in my face. Old Job nodded assent, coughed, and carefully wiped his gold-rimmed spectacles. I had noticed, in spite of my own confusion, that the cashier was dejected and nervous; his voice was husky, his hand trembled as he rubbed the dim glasses, and there was an unwonted moisture in his round blue eyes. As I followed Job into the inner parlour, where the merchants usually sat during business hours, I marvelled much what this wholly unexpected summons might portend. I had formerly been on terms of great and cordial intimacy with my employers; but for the last three months, my intercourse, with the senior partner in especial, had been strictly confined to business matters and dry routine. It was not that I had done anything to forfeit the good opinion of the firm. My employers had still the same confidence in me, the same regard for me, as heretofore; but there was an end, if not of friendship, at least of cordiality. This partial estrangement dated from the day when, with Emma Spalding smiling through tears and blushes at my side, I had ventured to tell the rich merchant that I loved his only daughter, and that my love was returned. It is an old, old story. We were two young persons of the same country and creed, alike in tastes and education, and in other respects, wealth excepted, not so ill matched; and we were together on a foreign shore, among strange people. We had been suffered to associate familiarly together, to read poetry, sing duets, and so forth; for Emma had no mother to watch against the approach of poverty-stricken suitors, and Mr. Spalding was a proud man, and not given to suspicion. Hence we glided—as millions of couples have done before, and will again—down the smooth rose-strewn path that leads from friendship to love I am sure of one thing: it was not my employer's wealth, or the idea of Emma's probable expectations from her father—who had but two children, a son and a daughter, between whom to divide the accumulations of a life spent in honourable toil—which allured me. But the time came when soft words and fond looks had to give place to an avowal of attachment. I spoke out to Emma, without premeditation; and, once across the Rubicon, other considerations, undreamed of as yet, came to beset me, mockingly. What would Mr. Spalding think of me? Surely, he could form but one judgment of the poor clerk, with no property beyond his pitiful savings, who had dared to entangle the affections of his master's daughter? My course was clear. I must tell him the truth, at whatever cost to myself.

I did so. The disclosure was hurried on by some slight unforeseen circumstance, as my proposal had been, but I was at least candid in my avowals. To do Mr. Spalding justice, he rejected my suit in as gentle and courteous a fashion as the harsh operation would admit of. But, cut to the heart, I withdrew from his presence, very, very wretched; and had for many days afterwards, serious thoughts of excluding myself from observation, becoming a solitary man, and leading a gloomy and moody life. Better thoughts, however, lying deeper within me, admonished me of the utter worthlessness of a purposeless existence, and of the utter contemptibility of the soul that can sink into it. And thus it fell out that I ceased to visit my employer as a private friend, and yet remained in his employ.

Was I mean-spirited for staying on thus? I cannot pretend to decide so nice a point, but I know that it was a great stimulant to me to have obtained a moral victory over myself, and some relief to the disappointment of my dearest hopes that I was still allowed to breathe the same air as Emma Spalding, to catch a glimpse of her sweet saddened face, were it but on the way to church, though for three weary months we never interchanged a word.

So I was not a little surprised when Job Wiginton summoned me to the presence of "the firm." My heart beat quickly as the old cashier turned the handle of the door. What could Mr. Spaulding want of me? I had kept the promise he had wrung from me; I had abstained from any intrusion, any unlicensed correspondence. Surely, surely he could not send for me merely to say that a rejected suitor was ineligible even as a servant, and that our

connexion must cease? In the larger of the two adjacent rooms, a room hung in Spanish fashion with stamped and gilded leather, and heavily furnished with dark mahogany from Honduras, I found the firm. Mr. Spalding, a tall thin grey headed gentleman, was pacing up and down the apartment in great agitation. Mr. Hausermann, a German, as his name implies, sat before a table covered with papers, ejaculating guttural exclamations of wonder from time to time, and with a look of hopeless perplexity in his fat pink face. The cashier entered along with me, and closed the door.

"Ach, mein Himmel!" muttered the junior partner: a hale, portly man, but of a flabby nature, morally and physically, compared with the energetic chief of the house: "ach! we were petter to have never peen porn, than live to see this!"

Job Wiginton gave a groan of sincere sympathy. I quickly perceived that something had gone wrong, and as quickly did I see that this mysterious something had no direct reference to my audacity in winning the heart of Emma Spalding. What was amiss? There is one grisly ghost that always haunts the imagination of the more intelligent subordinates of a commercial firm—Bankruptcy. But the house had been such a prudent house, so steady and well ballasted, had glided so demurely along in safe old-world groove, that it was rather ridiculed in consequence by the mushroom firms that daily arose or collapsed around us. But I had little time to think, for Mr. Spalding stopped in his walk, came abruptly up to me, and took me by both hands. 'George Walford," said the old merchant, with more emotion in his voice and features than he had ever shown before, "I have not been kind to you lately. You were a good friend to me—before—before——" and here he reddened somewhat, and ceased speaking.

I glanced towards Mr. Hausermann, but he looked so fat and helpless as he sat in his armchair, murmuring phrases in his native tongue, that I saw no explanation was to be looked for in that quarter. So I told Mr. Spalding, in as firm a tone as possible, that our mutual esteem had, I hoped, survived our intimacy, and that I still felt myself a faithful friend to him and his, and would gladly prove myself one.

"I thought so—I thought so," said the merchant, looking pleased for a moment; "you are a good lad, George, and that's why I come to you for help in my sore need, hard and harsh as you may have thought me the other day—when ——Never mind!"

"I was first to say it," exclaimed Mr. Hausermann. "'Let us call Shorge Walford,' say I. 'He has got ver goot prains; ver goot young man.'"

A quarter of a century spent among Anglo-Saxons had never taught Mr. Hausermann the English language in its purity. Indeed, his life, out of office hours, was spent entirely with Teutons like himself, who swarm all over America, and with whom he could enjoy German conversation, Rhine wine, and the black coffee of the fatherland. I should never get to the end of the interview if I described it verbatim, chronicling the broken sentences and vague talk of the junior partner, and the comments of Job Wiginton. The confidential cashier sympathised with the distress of his employers as a faithful dog might have done, and was about as likely to suggest a practical remedy. Mr. Wiginton was worthy of all trust; he was as close as wax and as honest as the day, but he was a mere machine for the casting up of sums, the balancing of books, and locking of safes. Mr. Hausermann was not much cleverer than the cashier; he was an admirable arithmetician, could detect an error of half a penny in a problem involving billions, and his penmanship was magnificent. But, with these attainments, he owed his present position in commerce, not to his abilities, but to the florins he had inherited, and to the talent and keenness of his English partner. It was from the chief of the house himself that I heard the following tale:—Mr. Spalding, as I have said, had but two children, Emma, and her brother Adolphus; his wife had died on the voyage from Philadelphia, and his affection centred in his boy and girl. Unluckily, Adolphus did not turn out well, was wild and extravagant, and squandered his liberal allowance among horse jockeys and gamblers. Mr. Spalding, strict with all the world besides, was rather lax and indulgent where his son was concerned. The young man was very good-looking and of pleasing address; he had been the darling of his dead mother; and the father was very patient and forbearing with him, for her sake. The youth went from bad to worse, got deeper into debt and evil company, seldom came home, and seriously impaired his health by a long course of excesses. All this I knew, for Adolphus was a clerk in the house, nominally at least, though he hardly ever occupied his stool in the office. But what I did not know was, that Adolphus Spalding, in his eagerness to settle a number of so-called debts of honour, had been led to rob his father. He had forged the signatures of Spalding and Hausermann to a cheque for thirty thousand dollars, payable at sight, and purporting to be drawn by the merchants on their bankers in New York. More than this: he had abstracted from his father's desk a Russia-leather pocket-book, containing bills and securities to a great amount, and this he had placed in the hands of the same vile associate who had undertaken to present the cheque at the counter of the New York bank.

"The scoundrel is gone northward already. He started last Tuesday, by the way of Panama, along with the mail," said Mr. Spalding. "You know the man, I dare say, for he was very notorious in the town—Joram Heckler."

"Dr. Joram Heckler!" I exclaimed, as I recalled to mind the dark clever face of the young man alluded to: a plausible, well mannered person, who had been sub-editor of a San Francisco newspaper.

"Yes, Doctor, or Colonel, Heckler," responded Mr. Spalding, with a bitter smile, "for it appears that he has assumed a military title on the journey back to the north. He possessed great influence over the mind of my misguided son; he was the tempter in this accursed robbery;

and I doubt not that he intends to appropriate the entire spoil to himself."

I now asked Mr. Spalding, as delicately as I could, how he had obtained his information.

It appeared that Adolphus, whose feeble frame, exhausted by hard living, was ill fitted to sustain the fierce excitement of the felonious act he had committed, had sickened of a fever, immediately after the departure of his accomplice.

"The wretched boy lies on his bed up-stairs, quivering betwixt life and death," said the father, with a faltering voice, "and in his delirium he has betrayed his guilt. His sister, who has watched at his bedside like an angel as she is, dear girl, she was frightened at his ravings of self-accusation. She called me, and with my own ears I heard the son I was so proud of—my petted boy—tell how he had cheated and plundered me."

The old merchant staggered to a chair, and I saw the tears trickle between the fingers with which he tried to hide the workings of his wrinkled face.

After a time he grew more calm. Then he developed his plan, in which broke out his habitual decision and force of character. Before all things, the honour of the house must be saved. The value of the money at stake (though a large sum) was trifling, compared to the disgrace, the loss of credit, the blot upon the name of Spalding. Yes, at any cost, the young man's shameful act must be hidden in darkness. The cheque must not be presented, the bills must not be negotiated. But how to prevent the tempter from realising the benefits of his ill-gotten booty! He was off—he was speeding towards New York by the quick Panama route; in a few weeks he would be there. No pursuit seemed possible. The delay till the start of the next mail would be fatal. I remembered the Pony Express, the swift overland mail whereby we Californian residents can most rapidly communicate with the civilised world, and I suggested this resource.

Mr. Spalding shook his head. "No, that would never do; I might send a despatch, no doubt, to stop the payment of the cheque. I might perhaps procure Heckler's arrest on his arrival in New York, but thence would spring inquiry, doubt, suspicion, and the whole black affair would creep into the journals before a week was out. No. I have but one hope, one chance: I must send a trustworthy person—I am too old to go myself—a trustworthy person to hasten to New York by the perilous route across the Rocky Mountains, and he must arrive before Heckler, and must get the papers from him by violence or stratagem. George Walford, you are the man I have selected."

"I, sir!"

I was stupified. Before my fancy rose, like a panorama, the long route, then but lately explored, that traversed the enormous continent from sea to sea: a route teeming with dangers. All I had ever heard or read of prairie travel, of famine, fire, the assaults of wild beasts, and of human foes more pitiless still, crowded on my memory at once. I thought of the vast distance, of the almost herculean fatigues to be undergone, of the icy barrier which the Rocky Mountains stretched across the track, as if to bar the progress of presumptuous man; and though I am no fainter of heart than my neighbours, I dare say my countenance expressed dismay and repugnance. Indeed, I am sure it did, for Mr. Hausermann groaned, and said, "Donner! what shall we to now?"

"Walford," said Mr. Spalding, "I don't wish to dissemble with you. I am asking you to incur the certainty of very great fatigue, hardship, and danger. I am asking you to risk life itself to save the honour of the house and that of my own family. I do not make such a request without proposing a proportionate reward.—There, hear me out! I don't offer you money for such a service. Come back successful, and you shall be a partner in the house of Spalding and Hausermann; and if you and Emma are still of the same mind three months hence——"

I trembled with joy as I interrupted my employer. "I'll go, sir, gladly and most willingly."

"That's a prave poy. I knew he would!" ejaculated the German; and the cashier rubbed his hands joyfully.

"When can you be ready to start?" asked Mr. Spalding.

"Directly. In half an hour, if you please."

"An hour will do," said Mr. Spalding, with a smile at my eagerness. "Bodesson shall be at the door by that time, with his carriage and his best horses. You must save your strength as much as you can for the prairie. You have a six-shooter, I know. Get ready what requisites for the journey will go into small compass. You shall have an ample supply of money—spend it freely, lavishly, and don't spare horseflesh or gold upon the way. I would give half my fortune to place you speedily on the pavement of New York. You are an ambassador with full powers, George, and your own wit and courage must carry you through. Now, you had better prepare for the road."

I lingered.

"Anything more to say?" asked the merchant, good-humouredly.

"If I could speak for a moment—just an instant—to Miss Spalding?"

"She is at her brother's bedside," replied the old man, hurriedly. "But—yes, you are right. You *shall* see her before you start."

I seemed to make but one step to the house where I lodged. I spent ten minutes in hastily arranging my belongings—and it is wonderful how much a man can condense into ten minutes when he is under the influence of strong excitement—charged my revolver, packed a few things in a small bag, and ran back like a greyhound. Mr. Spaulding gave me some fuller instructions, and handed to me a heavy parcel of gold and silver, as well as a bundle of bank-notes. I was to keep the bank-paper until I reached the civilized world; in the desert, my only hope would be to bribe in specie the half-tamed wanderers of the west. Mr. Spalding was still talking when Bodesson, one of the principal liverymen of San Francisco, drove his spanking pair of Spanish horses up to the door. Then

the merchant went up-stairs, and returned with his daughter. Dear Emma! she was pale and thinner than of old, but her eyes were bright and loving, and her words, full of hope and constancy, gave me fresh courage, and a resolve to do or die. Our parting was very brief. A few hurried whispers—a hasty renewal of the old vows and troth-plight—and for a moment I caught her in my arms and kissed her cheek, and in the next I was gone. I sat by Bodesson's side; the whip cracked; off flew the foaming horses along the street; and I looked back and waved a farewell in answer to Mr. Spalding's waving hand and Emma's handkerchief. Then we turned a corner, and darted along the road.

Bodesson was well paid, and he kept the mettled horses at their work over many a mile of ground. I seemed to start cheerfully, and under good auspices. My heart was full of hope. The gay French Creole by my side was a merry companion; he sang Canadian songs, whistled, chirruped to the bounding bays, and chattered incessantly.

"Monsieur was going to the prairies! Ah, très bien! The prairies were ver intéressantes, ver much so. But monsieur must take care when he got there—must not stir from the protection of ze dragoons, or les sauvages, ze ferocious Indians would carry off monsieur's cheveux—what you call scalp!"

So the Frenchman prattled on. He believed I was going to Salt Lake City on business, and never doubted that I should voyage with a caravan under escort of the States dragoons. What would he have said if he had known that I was to traverse that land of danger and hunger *alone?*

My journey to the eastern border of California was not remarkable enough to justify me in dwelling here on its details. Spending money freely, I was able to proceed almost entirely in wheeled carriages more or less rude, and I contrived to push along over sorry roads at a respectable pace. I slept in the vehicles during the dark hours, snatching a broken slumber as best I could, in the midst of jolting and swaying. Sometimes even a bribe could not induce my Mexican or American drivers to risk the perils of a stony road at night, and then I recruited my strength by rest, but was always ready to start at cock-crow. I knew well what was before me, and that all the fatigue I endured was child's play to what was in store. I had been on the prairies before—those at least which lie east of the Rocky Mountains. Mr. Spalding was well aware that I was a good horseman, expert in the use of fire-arms, and of a robust constitution. These are not the common attributes of a clerk, but I had not been bred to the desk. My father had been esteemed rich, till at his death, in embarrassed circumstances, I had been left to battle with poverty as I might; I had kept hunters at Oxford, and had been passionately fond of field sports. I had kept up the habit of taking brisk exercise, and now I was about to find the benefit of trained muscles and robust health. I did not disguise from myself that I was embarking on an enterprise full of risks. I might starve in the desert, whitened as it was by the bones of many an emigrant. I might perish miserably in one of those fires that rush like flaming serpents through the boundless sea of grass. And if my scalp did not blacken in the smoke of some Indian wigwam, fever or sheer fatigue might make an end of my life and hopes at once. Or, I might reach New York too late. It was gall and wormwood to me to think that Joram Heckler was pressing on towards the north with all the speed of a fast steamer. The very thought made me bound and stamp my foot on the floor of the rude mail-cart, as if I could quicken my progress by such a gesture. How I prayed that contrary winds might delay the packet on its passage from Aspinwall to the Empire City!

I reached Carson City on the border of the desert, and there I made a brief halt that I might prepare for the coming effort. I was perfectly well aware that the most dangerous and difficult part of the road was that lying between California and the Mormon settlements. Once beyond the Utah territory, I might well hope to escape the arrows and the tomahawk of the savage. I found Carson full of returning emigrants, diggers going back with their pelf to the Atlantic states, Mormon converts, and traders who had emptied their waggons in Californian markets. These good folks were all waiting for the regular escort of national dragoons, under whose guard they were to travel. It was impossible for me to move so slowly, and I accordingly bought a bag of sun-dried beef, another of parched corn, some blankets, and such matters, and a powerful horse handsomely accoutred with a bridle and saddle of Mexican make. I bought the latter from an American dealer who was mightily tickled at the idea of my making my way alone over the prairies. "I give you credit for your grit, sartainly, mister," said he: "it is good, and no mistake; but I guess you had better sleep upon the idea a few times more. Them Indian scalpers will lift your ha'r sure as hogs yield bacon. Won't you believe me? Come along, then, and ax another man's opinion!" And he dragged me towards a sort of tavern, the porch of which was crowded by men and women, French, Spanish, German, Yankee, and mulatto, all of whom were gathered round a lathy dark-haired young fellow in a trim half-military dress, that would have passed for that of a policeman but for the red flannel shirt and Mexican sombrero he wore. This man had keen mobile features, and was hardened by constant work and weather into little more than muscle and bone; he wore spurred boots and thick "savers," and was cracking a whip as he gaily chatted with the crowd, who laughed at his wit in a way that proved him a prime favourite. He was, in fact, one of the salaried riders of the "Pony Express," ready to start with a bag of despatches, the instant the courier from San Francisco should arrive with it.

"Yes, colonel; yes, galls," I heard him say; "I'm downright sorry to leave, but duty is duty, ain't it? If the Indians don't rub me out——"

"Rub you out, Shem? Catch a racoon asleep!" cried one of the rider's admiring friends.

"Waal!" said Shem with a modest voice, but a boastful twinkle in his restless eye, "the varmints have tried a time or two, but they've found Shem Grindrod rather a tough nut to crack, they have. When a chap's Kentucky bred, real right down hard hickory, 'taint so easy to lift his ha'r as——Service to ye, stranger!"

For his eye had lighted on me.

"Shem," cried the horse-dealer, "here's a gentleman wants to cross the parara, all alone, on hossback, Broadway fashion. What do you say to that?"

There was a general laugh. Shem took off his hat with mock respect.

"Whoop!" he cried. "If that ain't clear grit in the down-easter dandy! You'll see snakes, mister, I reckon. There's no accommodation for gen-teel persons, and you'll jest get your hoss stole, or chawed up by the wolves, and you'll lose yourself and die for want of a dinner, if you don't fall in with the Injuns—and if you do, Jehosaphat!"

All this would have been provoking to some men, but I knew the American character too well to be out of temper. Shem evidently took me for a presumptuous townsman, plunging wantonly into the lion's mouth, and was good-naturedly discouraging my rashness. With some trouble, I drew him apart, and commenced a private conversation. I told him that I was bound for the eastern states, that my business was imperative, but that if he could help me I would pay him most liberally for the aid rendered. For I had formed a crude idea that if I could procure the privilege of using the relays of spare horses kept at the different stations on the route, for the use of the mail-bag riders, I might accomplish the most awkward part of the journey with great rapidity. Shem, however, though not ill-natured, dashed my hopes to the ground. Such a concession would be "agin all rule." The servants of the Express Company "darn't do it." It was not to be thought of. I must wait for the caravan.

I did not wait for the caravan, but set forth that very day. The people gave me a half ironical cheer as I rode out of the straggling street of Carson, but I saw the Yankee dealer shake his head and screw up the corners of his mouth, as if he considered me little better than a suicide.

There was no use in letting the grass grow under my feet, so I pushed briskly ahead. I was riding a powerful horse, one of those bred in Kentucky or Tennessee, and which will sell for a high price on the western border of prairie-land. To find the way in broad daylight was easy. There was a broad track made by the passage of countless wagons and beasts of burden. I had a compass, but I really did not need it. I covered many a weary league of ground in the course of that day's ride. Here and there, among the forked streamlets which were feeders of the Carson, I came to farms where I easily procured corn for my horse and food for myself. I had come to two resolutions: one, to economise my little store of jerked beef as much as possible; the other, to refuse all hospitable proffers of whiskey, being convinced that on water only could such trying work as that before me he accomplished. I kept on, with brief pauses, through the day, and held to the track as long as the moonlight served me, urging on my flagging steed to the very limits of his strength. Then, in the dark, I dismounted, took off saddle and bridle, hobbled my horse, and tethered him so that he had ample space to graze. Then, I lay down, wrapped in my blankets, pillowed my head on my saddle, and fell asleep with my weapons by my side.

I awoke with a start, in a pitch dark night, and could not well remember where I was. My horse was uneasy, and his abrupt motions had disturbed me. I heard a rustling in the long grass, a scratching, a pawing of light feet amongst the herbage, and a whining sound as of hungry dogs whimpering for food. Dogs? There were no dogs there. Wolves! And my horse, on whose security my life might depend, was trembling and bathed in perspiration. I had kindled no fire, apprehensive lest the light should attract some band of prowling savages; and now the Coyotés were gathering around us like flies about honey. For myself, I felt no fear: the wolf of America is very different from the "grey beast" of German forests or Pyrenean snows. But my poor nag was in danger, and his very tremors were adding perilously to the exhaustion of the long and hurried ride. I rose, and began groping about for brushwood. Luckily I was still in a well-watered region, where shrubs and undergrowth abounded, and where the gigantic cotton-wood trees reared their majestic forms beside the streamlets. I soon came upon a clump of brush, and cutting with my sharp and heavy knife as much as I could carry in both arms, I returned with it, and cleared a little space of the grass, which was long enough to be dangerous in the event of its catching fire. I then took out my tin box of lucifers, struck a light, and kindled a fire: though not very easily, for the heavy dew stood in great glistening beads on grass and shrub, and the moistened wood emitted many a cloud of pungent and dark smoke, before I could coax the sullen embers to burst forth in the required blaze. All this time, I had to give an occasional halloo, rattling a tin cup against the barrel of my revolver, for the purpose of intimidating the wolves; while it was necessary to pat and soothe by voice and hand the poor horse itself, which was tugging at the tethering-rope in a way that threatened to break it every instant. At last, to my great joy, the fire leaped up, red and cheery, its bright beams illumined a little radiant patch of prairie, and, hovering in the shadows on the edge of this illuminated spot, I saw the slinking coyotés, the smallest and most timid, but also the most cunning, variety of the wolf of America. Presently I flung a firebrand among the pack, and they vanished into the darkness, but for half an hour I could hear their howls of disappointment, growing fainter and fainter, as the distance increased. My horse was quieter after the disappearance of the wolves, and in about an hour I ventured to return to my blankets and my repose, after piling a fresh heap of brush on the steadily glowing fire. Not very long afterwards, a feeling of intense cold awoke me by slow degrees. I opened my eyes. The fire was low; its embers glowed crimson, fading gradually into blackness. Overhead was the dim sky, the vast host of stars having the peculiar pale and sickly hue which heralds the dawn. It was very cold. There was a rushing sound in the air, and the grass of the prairie was tossed to and fro in wild confusion; a strong wind was blowing—the norther. This was the first blast of the chilly north wind that annually sets in at the close of the unhealthy season in the south. It had a piercing and glacial effect, coming, as it did, from the Polar ice-fields, and across the Rocky Mountain range; but I gladly hailed it, for I remembered that it would be dead against the mail steamer that was breasting the waters of the Mexican Gulf with Joram Heckler and his plunder on board. I might beat him yet!

But the wind increased in force; it was blowing like a hurricane, and I shivered in spite of my warm poncho and blankets. My horse had lain down, and was trembling with cold. I was obliged to spare him a blanket; he was a "States" horse, swifter, but not so hardy and useful for prairie travel as the mustangs of the plains. The wind did not diminish as the sun rose, red and angry, and a new cause of alarm began to haunt me. I had heard of travellers utterly weatherbound for days among the prairies, on account of the fury of the resistless wind. And time was so valuable to me! I felt sick at heart as the chilly hours of early morning crept on, and almost despaired of success. I was benumbed and stiff; the dew had been turned to icicles by the sudden cold; and now every waving blade of grass seemed crested with a diamond, glittering and flashing in the level sun shine. By nine o'clock the wind began to abate; it slackened very gradually, and at half-past ten I considered that I might resume my journey. My breakfast was not a luxurious one; a mouthful of beef and parched maize, swallowed in the intervals of saddling my horse and rolling up my blankets. Then, I drew up the iron peg to which the halter was attached, rolled up the halter, lasso fashion, at my saddle bow, and mounted. I was less awkward in the every-day routine of prairie life than might be supposed, Years ago, before I entered Spalding and Hausermann's employ, I had spent some weeks in a frontier fort, as the guest of the officers of a United States Ranger regiment. I had accompanied my hosts on several hunts and scouting expeditions against hostile Indians, and had found some amusement in picketing my steed, lighting camp fires, and so forth: little dreaming that my whole earthly happiness would ever depend on my proficiency in such arts. As the sun rose in the pale blue sky, nature assumed a more cheerful appearance; the icicles and hoar-frost melted, and the air became merely bracing and agreeable, as the bitter cold passed away. On we went, following the plain trail of the waggon trains, up and down the gently rolling slopes of the undulating prairie. I noticed with some dismay that my horse was no longer the mettled creature that had pranced so gaily out of Carson the day before. At first he certainly answered my voice and the pressure of my knee, by stepping out gallantly; but after a while he began to flag. bore heavily on the bit, and required a frequent touch of the spur. It was clear I had taxed his powers too severely on the previous day. He was going weakly under me, in a spiritless way that spoke volumes. What was I to do? I had plenty of money, but money cannot prove a talisman in the wilderness. There was not a farm between the place where I stood and the Great Salt Lake itself. My only chance in procuring a remount, lay in meeting some one who would sell me a steed, and this was far from a certainty I was chewing the cud of bitter reflections when I heard the light tramp of a galloping horse behind me. Quickly I turned my head, and saw a booted rider dashing gaily along over the swells of the prairie; his trim coat, half opened, showed a red flannel shirt; and his Mexican sombrero was bound with a cord of tarnished gold. He had a revolving carbine pistol at his saddle-bow, and at his side hung from his shoulder-belt his leathern despatch-bag. It was my acquaintance of yesterday—Shem Grindrod.

"Mornin', stranger!" he called out, cheerily; "I didn't skear you, yesterday, it seems, by my yarns about Injuns. 'Twas Gospel truth, for all that. Camped out, I reckon! Your hoss does look a little the wuss for wear, mister, though. You've pushed eim a goodish stretch, you have.'

We rode on for some distance side by side. My poor horse was inspired to do his best by the presence of the other norse, and together we sped over the country: my steed trotting, Shem's mustang galloping, for Spanish-American horses have but one pace when urged beyond a walk. Shem was much more kind and even polite in his manner than on the previous day. He told me, bluntly, that he respected a fellow that proved himself a man, but that what he hated worse than copperhead snakes was a Broadway dandy giving himself adventurous airs. My horsemanship had won Shem's esteem, and he sympathised heartily with me when he saw that I was really bent on crossing the dessert at any risk.

"Your hoss is a good bit of stuff, mister," said he, "but I'm afraid he's pretty nigh used up for one while. Now you listen to me. The best thing you can do is to buy a mustang fust chance you get. There'll be hunters passing south, and p'raps they'll trade. When you get right out among the plains, you stick to the trail well, and if a grass fire blinds it, you take your compass and bear up for east by north. Keep that pistol of yourn ready, and if you do see Injuns, keep cool. Don't waste a shot. Every round bit of lead is worth a life on the parara. Good-by, wish you luck."

Shem headed his horse for one of the Express stations, a little lonely block-house, with a stockaded yard, which was garrisoned by a few of his comrades, and where a relay of fresh horses was kept. I looked wistfully at the block-house and the well-stocked corral, and then turned away with my tired steed to resume my weary travel.

I knew that early in the afternoon I should reach another station of the same kind, and there I meant to apply for refreshment and shelter, in case my horse should knock up altogether. Before I had gone a mile, I saw my friend Shem, on a fresh steed, scouring the plain. He waved his hand, and gave me a cheer of recognition, and I looked after him enviously as he flew like an arrow up the slope, and vanished in the distance. By good luck, however, I almost instantly encountered a party of white men, the first travellers I had seen. These turned out to be three trappers returning from Oregon, with a fair stock of peltry loaded on two mules. They were all well mounted on "Indian ponies," and one of them led by a lariat a powerful and shapely mustang, whose bright eye and wide nostrils matched well with his wiry limbs. He had been captured on the plains, not two months before, one of a wild herd; but he was sufficiently broken in to be useful in prairie fashion. I struck a bargain with the trapper, by which my exhausted but more valuable quadruped was bartered for the half-wild mustang; the trapper also receiving four gold eagles. The arrangemen was mutually satisfactory, and as the ta l Kentuckian helped me to shift my saddle and bridle to the spotted nag I had just acquired, I saw his eyes twinkle with self-congratulation.

"One word of advice, colonel," said the trapper, as I placed the gold in his hard brown hand; "keep your eyes skinned as you go along, and don't let the cussed Redskins double upon you. There's Indian sign about, there is. I saw the print of a moccasin, down yonder by the spring, where the Indians never come for any good, mister. You mind—Utahs ain't to be trusted, and Shoshonies are worse. As for Rapshoes, Heaven help you, colonel, if they ketch you alone? There's Indians about. I smell 'em."

"I wish you'd got a good rifle on your shoulder, mister," said another, as I mounted; "six-shooters is very handly tools, but nothing sickens the Indians like a good five-foot bit of holler-iron, that air true."

I took leave of these good fellows, who wished me a safe journey in the heartiest way, though evidently disbelieving in the likelihood that a "greenhorn" could carry his property and scalp safe across the desert. The mustang was fresh, and darted along at that untiring though not very speedy gallop which animals of that hardy race can maintain for a very considerable time. We made capital progress: the country grew drier, and the grass shorter, and the swampy bottoms and trickling brooks were fewer. I met with no adventure, except that my new purchase put his foot into an outlying burrow, as we skirted a "village" of prairie dogs, and gave us both a roll on the turf; but we were unhurt, and I had luckily kept my grasp of the bridle, or I should have lost my horse. Once I thought I saw something hovering on the edge of the horizon, but whether savages, buffaloes, or wild horses, I could not determine. After riding several miles I came to a place where the trail dipped suddenly into a low tract of alluvial earth, intersected by a stream of some magnitude, and shaded by a belt of lofty cotton-wood trees. I traced here the fresh footprints of a horse which must just have passed, for the bruised grass had but partially risen around the edges. "Crack, bang!" went the sharp report of fire-arms ringing from the thicket below, and with the reports mingled the horrid war-whoop of the savage. Grasping my pistol, I dashed in among the trees, and beheld poor Shem Grindrod, bleeding, reeling in his saddle, and beset by a party of six or seven Indians, mounted, and in their hideous panoply of war. Shem had been pierced by three arrows: was fainting with loss of blood; but he fronted the savages boldly, and one Indian lay at his feet, rolling in the agonies of death. My arrival changed the current of the fight; two rounds from my revolver, the second of which laid low a muscular barbarian, smeared with yellow ochre, who was pressing on Shem with an uplifted tomakawk, sufficed for their discomfiture. Probably they took me for the advanced guard of a party of whites. At any rate, they fled at speed across the plain.

I was just in time to break Shem's fall, as the poor fellow dropped from his saddle, feebly murmuring, "Thank ye, mister. You've saved my scalp, any way, if 'twas just too late to save ——." His voice was hushed here, and he fainted in my arms.

There was a metal flask of whiskey dangling at the mail-bag rider's saddle-bow, along with his blanket and havresack; I hastily unscrewed the stopper, and contrived to force a few drops into the mouth of the wounded man. Then, I tore my cravat into strips, and with it and my handkerchief tried to bind up the hurts Shem had received, after vainly attempting to withdraw the barbed arrows. Two of the injuries were mere flesh wounds, more painful than dangerous; but the third was of a serious character: the shaft was imbedded in Shem's side, though the hemorrhage was trifling in appearance when compared with the abundant flow of blood from the other injuries. In about a couple of minutes Shem revived sufficiently to look up. I was touched by the gratitude his eyes expressed. Probably, poor lad, he had received but a scanty share of kindness in his scrambling life.

"Do you suffer much pain from the arrow wounds?" I asked "Take a drop more of the whiskey; it will give you strength, and if I can once help you to proceed as far as the blockhouse——"

"'Tain't no manner of use, stranger, my duty to ye, all the same," replied the rider, after swallowing a small quantity of spirits "I've got my finish at last. A chap that's fit in the border fights ever since he could squint along a gun, don't need no doctor to tell him when he's got goss, *he* don't."

I could not disguise from myself that Shem was right. His face showed a ghastly change; it was ashen white, pinched, and thin; while the lips twitched, and the eyes had acquired that peculiar eager glance, and restless craving brightness, which we never notice except in those over whom death hovers But I tried to cheer the poor fellow; succeeded in stanching the blood that flowed from his arm, transpierced by

two of the iron-tipped reeds; and begged him to keep up his hope and courage.

"'Tain't worth wasting words upon, mister," gasped Shem; "I knowed I'd my call; onst I felt the cold and the rankling pain that follered the smart of that cussed arrow in my ribs. I'm jest bleeding to death, inwardly, I am, and all the surgeon chaps in the States couldn't help me, no, nor yet the cleverest bonesetter in the pararas. But you cheated the curs out of my scalp, stranger. They had a hanker to get this child's ha'r, they had, to dance round in their darned village, them Shoshonies. My! How the squaws will jeer and mock 'em when they go back empty-fisted, and leavin' two of the pack behind 'em, too!" And Shem, with death in his face and at his heart, actually laughed. He had to catch painfully at his breath before he spoke again. "Stranger, it's an ill wind blows nobody any good. You hark to me. What I couldn't give you, nouther for dollars nor axin', you'll get now. Go on to the station; take this here mail-bag along; give it 'em, and tell 'em the rights of what's chanced. They'll turn out fast enough, I'll warrant, and they'll put me under the turf afore the wolves pick my bones. And another rider must go on with the bag. And tell 'em 'twere my dyin' wish, they'd give you a fresh hoss at each block, and so let you go with the rider, and push ahead. The Co. won't be riled at the breach of rules—seein' you saved the bag, let alone my scalp, and——".

He broke down here. I was quite melted at the unselfish thoughtfulness of this poor dying creature, this untaught, half-wild frontiers-man, who could care for my speedy journey while his own vital breath was trembling on his livid lips. I gave him a third sup of whiskey, begging him to let me know if I could communicate his last wishes to any distant friend or relation.

"There's a gal that lives to Hampton Town," said Shem, almost in a whisper, "the darter of a dealer that trades in mules, she be; and Ruth and I——Oh, 'tis a pity the wedding day were put off, cause the Co. gives pensions to wives, but none to sweethearts, and Ruth's father met with misfortins in trade, and she'd ha' been glad of a few dollars a year, poor thing!"

I asked his sweetheart's name, for, as I assured him, I felt certain that the house of Spalding and Hausermann would befriend her for his sake, if through the service I had rendered Shem I were really enabled to do my errand with a success otherwise unattainable.

"Ruth Moss," said Shem, in his weak voice; "that's her surname and given name. She's a good girl, pretty and good, is Ruth, and only too tender a flower for a rough borderman like me; goes to chapel reg'lar, and writes like a print book."

He then begged that I would send to Ruth a certain knot of ribbon which he had received from her as a keepsake, or merely snatched in a lover's whim, I do not know which; at any rate, I found it carefully wrapped in deerskin, in the bosom of his dress, but ah! with a deep dark stain of blood marring the gay blue of the silk. The arrow had passed nearly through that humble love-token. Shem further prayed me, that as I passed by the Round Pond Station, between Fort Bridge and Red Creek, I would tell his old father, Amos Grindrod, that he, Shem, "had died like a man."

"The old man'll be cut up, I'm afraid," murmured Shem, whose eyes were getting dim; " but he'll be glad to know my ha'r wan't lifted. Tell him I were wiped out by the band of Mad Buffalo, the Shoshonie. 'Twar Mad Buffalo hisself that sent the arrow through me, just as I kivered him with the carbine. The shunk! Many a noggin of drink I've given him when he come tradin' to the fort. But there war a grudge atween him and me, and he's ped it; but let him mind how he ever comes within range of old Amos Grindrod's rifle !"

Shem was anxious to know whether the Indian I had shot was quite dead, and what painted device his half-naked body bore. His own glazing eyes could not distinguish; but when I described the yellow ochre barred with white, he said it must be the "Little Owl," one of Mad Buffalo's best warriors. The other Indian was of slighter make, and daubed with black and vermilion. Both were stone dead. Shem asked me, half timidly, if I would be so good as repeat "a bit of Scripture." He had not been much of a chapel-goer, but Ruth had "got religion," and his mother, too, had been "a Christian woman," as he quaintly observed. I knelt beside him and held up his head as I uttered aloud the words of a brief and simple prayer, such as little children are taught to lisp with their innocent lips; and once or twice I heard the husky tones of the dying man repeat the words. But there was a strong shiver through his frame, and poor Shem Grindrod was dead before the prayer was prayed out.

About an hour later, I rode up to the station, mounted on my own horse, and leading Shem's by the bridle,

"Halloa! pull up, pull up, or I'll plug ye, sure as my name's Bradshaw!" shouted a stern voice through a loophole of the lonely blockhouse. And I saw the long clouded barrel of a frontier rifle pointing in my direction. I halted, of course.

"That's one of our hosses," cried a second voice; "the critter's stole it, I reckon. What is he?"

"I am a friend," I called out: "a traveller from California. Let me come in, and I will explain all."

The garrison held a short but animated debate. One man avowed his belief in the truth of my story, another broadly hinted that I might turn out a "renegade" or "white Indian," that I merely wanted to open the doors of the fortress to my ferocious allies, ambushed somewhere hard by, and that it would be as well to shoot me, as a provisional act of prudence. But the majority carries the day in America; and, luckily for me, the majority decreed my admission. Loud was the surprise, and sincere the sorrow with which the little garrison received the news of their comrade's murder. Three of the men caught up such rude tools as they possessed, and, slinging their rifles,

prepared to take the "back trail" to the spot where the unfortunate young man's body lay, and where his remains would be hastily laid in earth, after the custom of the frontiers. Another hurried, with all the instinct of discipline, to saddle a horse for the purpose of carrying forward the mail-bag which poor Shem had resigned only with his life. This rider was the most affected of the group, by the melancholy tidings I had brought. He would have preferred to be one of those who were to lay his old associate beneath the prairie turf, but this could not be. He was "next for duty," he said, simply, with tears standing in his hardy eyes. So, he hurried to equip himself and steed for the perilous road. I now ventured, rather timidly and awkwardly, to prefer my request for the accommodation of fresh relays of horses along the rest of the route, speaking as modestly as I could of my own preservation of the despatches. The men looked puzzled as they scrutinized me and weighed my demand. One of them, he who had taken me for a renegade white in the Indian interest, gave me a piercing glance, and gruffly said, "How do we know he ain't been bamfoozling us with a pack of lies? He may have murdered Shem, ye see, jest to get a remount, and——"

"You jest shut up!" thundered, in tones of deep indignation, the rider who was to carry on the mails. "You oughter to be ashamed of that tongue o' yourn, Jethro Summers. Here's a gentleman, and what's more, an honest chap, has fit by poor Shem's side, has saved his scalp from them Shoshonies, and brought on the bag for us, and you're to insult him with your mean talk. See! his hoss is fresh, and he's brought in Shem's hoss; and you to go telling him he'd murder a white Christian to get a lift. It's a burnin' shame, Jeth Summers!"

"'Tis, 'tis!" exclaimed the other two men. "Did ye ever know a darned renegade look a chap in the face, bold and honest, like the colonel, there? He's a good chap, is mister; and if ever he wants a friend in a rough-and-tumble fight, we're his men, sure as minks can swim."

The trio shook hands with me with genuine warmth. Now, when the iron was hot, was the time to strike. I therefore made an energetic appeal to them to supply me with horses, assuring them that my whole prospects and happiness, as well as those of others, depended on my speed. They listened with interest; but when I concluded with the words, "Shem Grindrod wished it; he bade ask it of you, as he lay dying," the game was won. To be sure, the one ill-conditioned member of the community grumbled out something about "soft sawder, breach of rules, cunning Yankees, and dismissal." But the tall rider cut him short, by affirming with an oath, that "if the Co. chose to ride nasty on such a point, after the stranger's services, why the Co. was a mean scamp, and he wouldn't serve 'em for one." I did not at first exactly comprehend this frequently-recurring phrase of the "Co.," and was disposed to regard it as the name of some over-looker, or superintendent, but afterwards discovered that this monosyllabic impersonation meant the Express Company.

"Look sharp, mister. You shall have a mount, but there's time lost a'ready, and we shall have to ride whip and spur. Come and pick a nag out of the corral. There's a brindled mustang your saddle will fit like his skin. The roan's best, but his back's rubbed raw. Ask Jonas to give you some beef and biscuit: we shan't pass many hot-els, that air positive. Charge that revolver o' yourn, colonel; I see two bullets a missing. Have a horn of whiskey —old Monongahela! No! Do be spry with the saddle, you Jeth—a man should help in a case like this. Easy, mister, with the bridle—the mustang bites—so! We'll take care of your nag, and you will find him as sleek as a slug, if you come back our way. Good-by, boys!"

So saying, the impatient rider finished his preparations, sprang to his saddle, waved his repeating carbine over his head, and set off at furious speed. I followed as rapidly as I could, shouting a farewell to those left behind, who were on the point of starting for the place where poor Shem was lying beside the corpses of his copper-hued foes, stiff and stark.

The brindled mustang was fat and lazy, compared with the nimble cream-coloured pony on which my guide was mounted. It took all my exertions to overtake 'Demus Blake, whose name was probably Aristodemus, though thus curtailed by usage. We rode at a tremendous pace.

"Larrup your beast, colonel," cried the rider, "we're woful behind. Don't be stingy with the spur-iron, for that brindle does allays skirk when he can. Mind—'ware the sappy ground, where you see them clubby mosses! Jordan! they'd take a hoss up to the girths, and there you'd stop, like a tree'd coon. Push on, sir. Rattle him across them riv'lets: not that a parara hoss can jump like the critters from the U-nited States."

It struck me that 'Demus Blake was bawling and flogging in this excited way, for no other purpose than to quiet his own nerves, and drown care. I was confirmed in this view by the fact that, after six or seven miles had been swallowed up by the rapid career of our foam-flecked steeds, the rider reined his horse into a steady hand-gallop.

"There, mister," said he, "we'll go quiet now. I feels kiender easier under my left ribs. Tell'ee, colonel, little as you think it, to look at such as me, I was as near making the bigest baby of myself—there, I was! Poor boy Shem! I knowed him, sir, oncommon well, and on-common long. We played about together, when we were as high as a ramrod, in Pequottie village, nigh to Utica, in old Kentuck. And when old Amos and my daddy, Jonathan Blake, calculated to move west, they chose the same location. Sad news for old Amos—a white-haired old chap now, but pretty tough, too. He's at Brown's Hole—no, at Round Pond—trading for peltry. I wouldn't care to have the tellin' on him."

The rider was silent for a good while after this. He did not speak again till I paid a merited tribute to Shem's courage. I had found him, I said, fronting seven Indians like a stag at bay. The frontiers-man's eye glittered proudly:

"A brave boy, sir, I was with him, first fight—that is, Shem's first, cause I'm two year an older man. 'Twarn't hereaway. South of Fremont's Pass it wur, and bloody Blackfoot Indians war the inimy, three to one, on'y they'd no fire-arms. 'Twarn't child's play that day, mister!" The backwoodsman expanded his broad chest, while his nostrils dilated, and his lips tightened, as he recalled the arduous struggle long past.

He was a much stronger man than Shem, of a spirit less gay and lightsome, but not without a certain amount of rude practical poetry in his disposition. He knew Shem's sweetheart: a very nice-looking girl, of rather a quiet, subdued, and pious nature. "Not too common on the border, nouther, where even gals mostly has a spice of the wild-cat, but, mebbe, that pleased Shem."

Of the distress in store for old Amos Grind-rod: a hunter, once renowned for his prowess and skill, whether in warfare or the chase: Blake spoke feelingly and with deep conviction.

"'Twill shorten the old man's days, sir, but it's lucky the old woman's not alive to hear it: she was that tender of Shem, if his finger ached she'd flutter like a robbed hen. Good old soul she was, Mrs. Grindrod, and nursed my old mother when she took the fever in that murderin' swamp."

Honest 'Demus had too much innate good-breeding to be inquisitive as to the purport of my unusual journey. In this respect, as in some others, he far surpassed in tact and polite-ness many an accomplished citizen in varnished boots and satin vest. But he offered me some well-meant advice.

"Take it coolly," said he, "and don't flurry yourself, colonel. You've got more colour in your cheeks than need be, and your hand was as hot, when I shook it, as a bit of deer-meat toastin' over the fire. I don't know as you ain't right, shirking the whiskey, though 'tis food and comfort to such as me. But a smart touch of fever would tie you by the leg, stranger, so don't fret overly, and sleep all you can. As for Injuns, they'll hardly trouble two white men, when there's nouthin' to be got but a kipple of nags that can be bought for a cast of the lasso, or larist. The emigrant trains is different, for the Red devils scent plunder in the waggons, and only the dragoons skear 'em. Twar spite med the Mad Buffalo fall on Shem Grindrod. Shem give him a coat o' tar and turkey feathers one night, at Bridger's Fort, when the Injun got so drunk with whiskey some rascal sold him, he lay like a hog on the ground. They never forgive, them Injuns. Shoshonies have no pity, compared to the savages east of the Rocky Mountains. Keep a look-out for outlying war parties, mister, when you get to the mountain parks. Crows will take hoss and clothes; Blackfeet allays hanker arter ha'r!"

I took my guide's well-meant advice, and endeavoured to get through the journey as phlegmatically as might be. I snatched every opportunity of repose, if only for a few minutes, while the reeking saddles were being shifted to the backs of fresh horses; and it is wonderful how much refreshment I at times derived from a nap so brief as not much to exceed the traditional "forty winks." More than once, my companion said to me, "Colonel, you're about dropping with sleep. Shut your eyes, if you like, and give me your reins. I'll guide both horses, and you can't hardly roll out of that cradle o' yourn." And, indeed, the deep Mexican saddle of demipique cut, which I had luckily provided on starting, was admirably adapted, with its lofty pommel and cantle, to the use of a dozing equestrian. Curious spells of slumber those were, when my head would nod like that of a porcelain mandarin, and my eyelids droop as if weighted with lead, and when, after a few minutes, I would start up, broad awake, as my mustang stumbled over broken ground. Once —it was while 'Demus Blake was still with me —I had a long and most delicious period of slumber, uninterrupted by jerks or concussions; and when I awoke, quite a new man, and revived to an extent at which I now wonder, I found myself supported by the strong patient arm of my conductor, who had been galloping by my side for miles, managing both bridles with his disengaged hand. "I thought it would fresh you up, colonel!" said the brave fellow.

Not all my mentors throughout that phantom ride across prairieland were as frank as Blake, nor as merry as Shem. But the mail-bag riders turned out good fellows in all main points, and I can safely say that I found but two or three surly or ill-natured persons among all those who garrisoned the block-houses: while fortunately it fell to my lot on no occasion to be accompanied by one of these. In the prairie, as in the world at large, I found good-feeling the rule, cynicism or malice the exception, though I am bound to say that the ill-conditioned individuals made twice as much noise and stir as their more amiable mates. The first start had been difficult, but at each succeeding station I received my remount without much delay or parley. The "privilege of the post" was conceded to me, while I was always welcome to a share of the rations in each little community. On the whole, I found the men cheerful in their strange isolation. They were liberally paid and not ill-fed, and they looked forward to a pension in the event of becoming crippled by some Indian hatchet-stroke or arrow-shot. Planted in the wilderness, with the prospect of being presently encompassed by deep drifts of snow, over whose frozen surface the wolves would come to howl and scratch at their doors, like dogs seeking admittance, they were in fair spirits and undismayed. Their habitual talk was of the wild adventures that formed the every-day life of that frontier of Christendom; of Indian stratagems and cruelty, of panthers and "grizzlies," pronghorns and buffaloes. Several of them had consorted familiarly with the painted tribes of the desert, and spoke sundry Indian dialects as fluently as their mother tongue. I found these hardy men kind hosts enough; they would hush their talk, not to disturb me as I lay down on a heap of skins and blankets, to sleep, while

the guide saddled the horses; and they soon ceased to ridicule my apparently capricious refusal of whiskey. "Mebbe the colonel's right!" (Colonel is the Western title of courtesy), they would say in their blunt politeness. Once I found the inmates of a station, built on swampy ground, quite helpless and prostrate with fever. The fever had abated when the healthy norther began to blow, but the poor fellows were cramped with pains, and very feeble, and only one of the party could crawl about to cook and feed the fire. I had need to fix my mind on the reward of success, on the distant goal glittering far ahead, for it was no light task that I had undertaken. The thought of Emma nerved me, and I felt an Englishman's dogged resolve to win, to fight on, and to break sooner than bend. But the fatigues of that journey surpassed all my conceptions. By day and night, under a glaring sun or through the frosts and cutting northerly winds, on we pressed, fording streams, threading the way through marshes, stumbling among the burrows of prairie dogs, or dashing across boundless plains. I almost learned to hate the long terraces of turf, the illimitable sweeps of dark green surface, the blue horizons, the swells of gently sloping earth, smooth enough for the passage of wheeled carriages. On we went, till the long grass, mixed with flowers and wild tufts of the flax-cotton, gave place to a shorter and crisper herbage, the true "buffalo grass" that the bisons love; or till water became scarce, and the sage plant replaced the blossomed shrubs of the west, and the springs were brackish, and here and there our horses' hoofs went cranching over a white stretch of desert, strewn with crystals of salt that glittered in the sun. We saw little of Indians, and of game still less. The latter, my guides told me, had been chiefly scared away, by the constant passage of emigrants. As for the savages, we sometimes saw the plumed heads, the tapering lances, and the fluttering robes, of a troop of wild horsemen, against the crimson sky of evening: but they offered us no molestation, and the riders said they were Utahs on the look-out for "buffler droves" returning from the south. Of the fatigue of that interminable ride, the aching joints, the stiffened sinews, the pains that racked my overstrained muscles, I can give no just idea. Still less can I convey any sense of the continual strain upon the intellect and the perceptive faculties, or how my brain grew as weary as my limbs.

I shall never forget the evening of my arrival in Salt Lake City, the capital of Utah territory, and New Jerusalem of the Mormons. I had been encouraged by the guides to look upon this town in the deserts as a turning-point in the journey, beyond which I should be in less peril from Indians, and after which a comparatively short ride would carry me to more civilised regions. But, to my surprise, I found the inmates of the station at Salt Lake City quite as lonely as, and more suspicious and moody than, in the far-off posts among the prairies. They were Gentiles in the midst of a fanatic population, wholly swayed by the hierarchy of that strange creed whose standard had been set up in the lawless wastes of the west. Nor was it long before I heard the cause of their dark looks and low spirits.

"Where's Josh Hudson?" asked the rider who had come with me, when the first greetings had been exchanged.

"Who knows?" answered the man addressed; "*I* don't. Seth said he went to the town, while I were in the corral with the horses. If so, all I can say is, he never come back."

"When was that, Seth?" asked the newly-arrived rider.

"Two days agone," answered Seth, as he scraped the surface of a half-exhausted quid of tobacco with his long sharp bowie-knife, "jest afore sundown."

"He's not deserted. Josh was too honourable to make tracks, that way," said the rider, confidently.

"Deserted! Not he. But that's what'll have to be put in the report—leastways, missin'," said Seth.

The rider looked Seth in the face, and drew his forefinger, with a meaning look, slowly across his own throat. Seth nodded.

"Least said, safest," said Seth, looking dubiously at me.

"Colonel's safe. You may speak afore him, same as myself, boys!" cried the mail-bag rider, who had come with me; "do ye mean them bloodthirsty Mormons——?"

"Whist, Jem! Whew! You'll get all our throats cut," cried the oldest man, starting up in great alarm; "there may be one of the brutes within earshot." He looked through the window, and opened the door, to satisfy himself that no eavesdroppers were near.

"I forgot," apologised Jem; "but about Josh Hudson?"

"I'm afeard," answered Seth, in a voice dropped almost to a whisper, "that he's gone for good. Josh was troubled about his sister, Nell Hudson, that jined the Mormons last winter, up in Illinoy, and was coaxed off, and is here, somewhere."

"Ah," said the listener, "I heerd as much."

"It's my belief," continued Seth, "that Josh got on this station a purpose to seek the gal out, and get her to go home to the old folks and the Church she were bred in. Mormons won't stand at."

"Ah?" said the guide Jem again.

"So, in short, Seth and me some think, we do," said the oldest of the group, "that Josh has been at his scoutin' onst too often, and met shanpip.'"

"Shanpip!" I repeated; "what is that?"

The man eyed me curiously. "Never heerd of 'Shanpip brethren,' then, harn't ye, mister? So much the best for you. P'raps you've heerd tell of Danites?"

I *had* heard, vaguely and obscurely, of that spiritual police of Mormondom, of those fierce zealots who obey their Prophet blindly.

"Then you have reason to fear that your comrade is——"

"Is lyin' under the salt mud of one o' them briny pools nigh to hand," interrupted the man,

"and not alone, nouther. Theer's been a many missin', that never went back to settlements nor on to Californey. And theer they'll lie hid, I reckon, till the Day of Judgment, when Great Salt Lake shall give up its dead, like the rest of the airth and waters."

I asked if an appeal could not be made to the Mormon elders themselves?

"'Twouldn't answer, colonel. Suppose I goes to-morrow to Brigham's own house, or Kimball's or any of their big men—elders, or angels, or high priests, or what not—and asks after Josh Hudson. Brigham's very mealy-mouthed, afraid the man's run away; what could be expected from a benighted Gentile, and that; gives his own account of it in preachment next Sabbath. P'raps one of 'em gives me a glass of wine or a julep, and mebbe it disagrees with me, and I die of it. You may stare, but didn't the States treasurer die that way, arter takin' refreshment at Angel Badger's house? And a pretty angel *he* be. P'raps I don't drink under a Mormon roof, and then, mebbe, I walk home late, and lose my way, or some other accident happens me—true as death, mister, on'y last week, and I passed Big Lick, I saw a dead woman's face looking up at me, all white and still, at bottom of the salt pool."

Thus far the elder man had spoken, but now Seth, who had evinced great uneasiness, jumped up with an oath, and cautiously opened the door. No one was listening.

"Tell'ee what," said Seth, "we'd best keep this discoorse close, till we're outside the territory. They're that sharp, Mormons, blessed if I don't think they're all ear. And if they get's a notion what we're sayin', the colonel won't never see New York, and I shan't never happen home to Montgomery agin. Indian Walker and his pesky Utahs mostly got a knack of tomahawking them as Mormons don't much like. And mebbe we'd meet other Indians, with blankets and red paint on their faces, jest like the real Utahs, and pretty sharp knives in their belts."

"Seth's right," said my former guide; "we don't want to set up any chaps to paint Injun on our account, as Angel Brown and Young Harris and the Danites did, when Martha Styles and Rachel Willis chose to go home to Illinoy—so, colonel, you get a snooze, and Seth, you needn't hurry about saddlin'—we've rode awful quick."

I was not sorry when day-dawn found me, after a hard gallop by moonlight, approaching the confines of the Mormon territory. The rest of the journey was unmarked by adventure. Hardships there were, but no great perils. We traversed a route on which the bleached bones of many horses and mules lay white and ghastly, and on which many a low turfen mound marked the last resting-place of an emigrant, or his wife or child, never to reach the Promised Land of Hope.

But provisions were more plentiful now, and water more regularly stored and easy of access, than when the expelled Mormons made their famous march across the desert, marking the untrodden route with graves. We narrowly escaped being smothered in the snow, in passing the outlet in the Rocky Mountains, and this was our last semblance of peril.

Previous to this, it had been my sad duty to tell old Amos Grindrod, whom I found at the Round Pond Station, of his son's death, and to commit to his care the bit of ensanguined ribbon that was to be returned to poor Shem's sweetheart. The old man tried to bear the tidings with the stoicism of those Indians among whom he had passed much of his life, and expressed great pleasure at hearing that Shem had "died like a Kentucky man, clear grit," and that I had come up in time to save his scalp. But in a few minutes, nature conquered. The old man's bronzed features worked and twitched, and tears trickled from his aged eyes, as he sobbed out, "Shem! dear boy Shem! 'twas I that oughter be dead, not he."

At last the weary ride was over: we had passed outlying farms guarded by a strong stockade, then the farms grew thicker and the stockades were dispensed with, and at last the roofs of a village, called by courtesy a town, came in view. Gladly did I dismount, gladly did I shake the hard hand of the last rider of the Express Company! Leaving that honest fellow puzzling over the cabalistic flourishes of a ten-dollar note I presented to him, I hired a pair-horse waggon of light build, and set off at once. The waggon bore me on until I exchanged it for a coach, the coach did me the same good office until I heard the snort of the steam-horse, and took my ticket by railway. How delicious, how snug and luxurious was such a mode of travel, after so much hard saddlework! Corduroy roads seemed smooth, and American railroads not in the least addicted to cause the trains to jerk or rock. The gliding motion was charming, and I made amends for lost time, by sleeping in a manner which provoked more than one fellow-traveller, eager to know my business and station in life.

I had already telegraphed to New York briefly thus:

"Has the Californian mail, viâ Panama, arrived?"

Briefer still was the answer:

"No."

That was right, so far. My toil was not yet purposeless. I might hope to be in New York before Dr., or Colonel, Joram Heckler. The victory, to be sure, was not yet won. The valuable papers remained in the scoundrel's keeping. But my presence in New York would be unsuspected by him, and any overt act on my part would have the effect of a surprise. I was too exhausted to devote myself to spinning air-drawn schemes for outwitting the intriguer. I should have need of all my faculties when the tug of war began, and I must sleep now. Sleep I did, over miles and miles, over leagues and leagues, of the iron way: resting obstinately, and being as passive as possible.

"Massa get out? Dis New York, sare."

Some one was shaking me by the arm: some one else held a lantern to my face. A black man and a white. The conductor, and a negro porter.

"I'm going to the Metropolitan Hotel. I want a hack: no luggage. Has the Californian mail arrived?"

"Yes, it has," said a newsvender, who stood by, with a heap of journals under his arm; "got all the news here. Herald, Tribune, Times. Which will you have?"

I bought one of the papers, and glanced at the list of arrivals viâ Panama. So much gold dust, so much bullion, distinguished European traveller, postmaster-general Signora Cantatini, Colonels Thom, Heckler, &c. The driver of the back-carriage was an Irishman, as usual, and, luckily, not a new arrival. He readily conducted me (at that late hour all other stores and shops were closed) to the emporium of a Jew dealer in ready-made clothes, who was willing to turn a cent even at irregular time. I purchased a new suit, linen, a portmanteau, and so forth, and shaved off my stubbly beard with razors supplied by the Jew, and before the Jew's private looking-glass. My driver drove quite a trim, ordinary-looking gentleman to the Metropolitan Hotel, instead of the shaggy flannel-shirted Californian who had first engaged him.

Before I engaged a room, I civilly asked the bookkeeper to let me look at the addresses of guests: I was expecting my brother, I said, from Albany. I took good care to say nothing of Heckler or California, and the bookkeeper had no suspicion that my voyages had commenced at any more remote spot than Philadelphia or Baltimore. Yes—Heckler's name was down.

I had guessed he would put up at the Metropolitan, for I had heard him mention the house approvingly in conversation. I hung about the bar and the staircases until I happened to hear that he had gone to bed. Then, I withdrew to think over my own plan of operations. I own I was puzzled. I tossed and tumbled uneasily on my pillow. While hurrying onward it had appeared as if I had but to arrive in time, and the difficulty was at an end; but now, what was I to do? The battle had yet to be fought. What should I do? In the morning, no doubt, Heckler would repair to the bank, to present the forged cheque, if not to get the bills discounted. I must stop him. But how? Should I go to the police, and return with the police myrmidons? Not to be thought of! Scandal, exposure, must follow such a step; nay, in the eyes of the law, Heckler might seem an innocent man, and I a false accuser. I next thought of confronting him boldly, and forcing from him, with a pistol at his head, if need be, the property of the firm. But this was too Quixotic a proceeding to be adopted in a first-rate hotel in New York. I was at my wits' end.

Heavens! What a smell of burning, and how stifling and thick the air! Smoke! The house is on fire. Up I sprang, and flung on my clothes in hot haste. "It's an ill wind that blows no one any good." I thought of Joram Heckler as I rang my bell to alarm the people.

"Fire! fire!" The awful cry broke upon the ears of the sleepers, like the trump of doom. Dark clouds of volleying smoke poured along the corridors, flecked here and there by thin ribbons of flame that licked the walls and floors like the tongues of fiery serpents. Shrieks were heard; doors were burst open; men, women, children, rushed out, half-dressed and screaming. There was panic terror and wild confusion. The fire gained ground, the smoke was blindingly thick, and all fled before it—all but myself. I steadily groped my way towards Joram Heckler's room. I knew the number, and where to find it. I knew that I risked my life, but the stake was worth winning at such a risk. I was very nearly suffocated as I pushed on, holding by the wall, into the thickest of the smoke. Some man, half-dressed, and winged by fear, came rushing by with extended arms, and nearly overturned me. He uttered a savage oath; the red glare of the fire fell on his face; it was Joram Heckler.

He did not recognise me, but dashed on, only mindful of his danger. Had he the papers with him? I thought not. I hoped not. That was *his* room then, the door of which was ajar, and into which the smoke was rolling. Not the smoke alone; I saw a thin red tongue of fire creeping in over the floor, beside the wainscot. I dashed in. My eyes smarted with the smoke, and I gasped for breath, but smoke and fire could not turn me now. Heckler's clothes and dressing-case were as he had laid them; the latter was open; no papers! His valise, too, lay open: no papers! I struck my forehead despairingly. He had them about him then? I was risking life idly. Emma was lost to me! The smoke choked me: the intolerably hot fire had gained the bed: valance and curtains were flaring high in a tall yellow pillar of flame. The subtle tongues of flame almost touched my feet. I must fly, if I would not perish. Outside, I heard the noise of the ingines and the cheers of the mob, and then the dash of water, as prodigious efforts were made to extinguish the fire.

I was staggering away, when I saw, peeping from under the bolster of the bed, a Russia-leather pocket-book. The rascal had forgotten it in his blind terror. The blazing curtains fell in fragments upon me, and my hands were a good deal scorched, but I rescued the precious prize. I tore it open. Yes, cheque and bills, all were there! Thrusting it into my breast-pocket, I left the room, and struggled as I best could down the passage. Dash after dash of water, flung from hand-buckets, had partially subdued the flames, and the firemen were gaining the victory. Half smothered, singed, blackened, but with a proudly beating heart, I forced my way down the heated and crowded staircase—reached the outer air, and fainted.

I have little more to tell. I am a partner in the firm: Emma is my wife; her brother recovered from his illness, and is now in another land, an altered and a penitent man. The house of Spalding, Hausermann, and Co. (I am Co.) have granted a pension to the poor girl who was to have been the bride of the luckless Shem Grindrod.

VI

PICKING UP MISS KIMMEENS.

THE day was by this time waning, when the gate again opened, and, with the brilliant golden light that streamed from the declining sun and touched the very bars of the sooty creature's den, there passed in a little child; a little girl with beautiful bright hair. She wore a plain straw hat, had a door-key in her hand, and tripped towards Mr. Traveller as if she were pleased to see him, and were going to repose some childish confidence in him, when she caught sight of the figure behind the bars, and started back in terror.

"Don't be alarmed, darling!" said Mr. Traveller, taking her by the hand.

"Oh, but I don't like it!" urged the shrinking child; "it's dreadful."

"Well! I don't like it, either," said Mr. Traveller.

"Who has put it there?" asked the little girl. "Does it bite?"

"No,—only barks. But can't you make up your mind to see it, my dear?" For she was covering her eyes.

"O no no no!" returned the child. "I cannot bear to look at it!"

Mr. Traveller turned his head towards his friend in there, as much as to ask him how he liked that instance of his success, and then took the child out at the still open gate, and stood talking to her for some half an hour in the mellow sunlight. At length he returned, encouraging her as she held his arm with both her hands; and laying his protecting hand upon her head and smoothing her pretty hair, he addressed his friend behind the bars as follows:

Miss PUPFORD's establishment for six young ladies of tender years, is an establishment of a compact nature, an establishment in miniature, quite a pocket establishment. Miss Pupford, Miss Pupford's assistant with the Parisian accent, Miss Pupford's cook, and Miss Pupford's housemaid, complete what Miss Pupford calls the educational and domestic staff of her Lilliputian College.

Miss Pupford is one of the most amiable of her sex; it necessarily follows that she possesses a sweet temper, and would own to the possession of a great deal of sentiment if she considered it quite reconcilable with her duty to parents. Deeming it not in the bond, Miss Pupford keeps it as far out of sight as she can—which (God bless her!) is not very far.

Miss Pupford's assistant with the Parisian accent, may be regarded as in some sort an inspired lady, for she never conversed with a Parisian, and was never out of England—except once in the pleasure-boat, Lively, in the foreign waters that ebb and flow two miles off Margate at high water. Even under those geographically favourable circumstances for the acquisition of the French language in its utmost politeness and purity, Miss Pupford's assistant did not fully profit by the opportunity; for, the pleasure-boat

Lively, so strongly asserted its title to its name on that occasion, that she was reduced to the condition of lying in the bottom of the boat pickling in brine—as if she were being salted down for the use of the Navy—undergoing at the same time great mental alarm, corporeal distress, and clear-starching derangement.

When Miss Pupford and her assistant first foregathered, is not known to men, or pupils. But, it was long ago. A belief would have established itself among pupils that the two once went to school together, were it not for the difficulty and audacity of imagining Miss Pupford born without mittens, and without a front, and without a bit of gold wire among her front teeth, and without little dabs of powder on her neat little face and nose. Indeed, whenever Miss Pupford gives a little lecture on the mythology of the misguided heathens (always carefully excluding Cupid from recognition), and tells how Minerva sprang perfectly equipped, from the brain of Jupiter, she is half supposed to hint, "So I myself came into the world, completely up in Pinnock, Mangnall, Tables, and the use of the Globes."

Howbeit, Miss Pupford and Miss Pupford's assistant are old, old friends. And it is thought by pupils that, after pupils are gone to bed, they even call one another by their christian names in the quiet little parlour. For, once upon a time on a thunderous afternoon, when Miss Pupford fainted away without notice, Miss Pupford's assistant (never heard before or since, to address her otherwise than as Miss Pupford) ran to her, crying out " My dearest Euphemia!" And Euphemia is Miss Pupford's christian name on the sampler (date picked out) hanging up in the College hall, where the two peacocks, terrified to death by some German text that is waddling down hill after them out of a cottage, are scuttling away to hide their profiles in two immense bean-stalks growing out of flower-pots.

Also, there is a notion latent among pupils, that Miss Pupford was once in love, and that the beloved object still moves upon this ball. Also, that he is a public character, and a personage of vast consequence. Also, that Miss Pupford's assistant knows all about it. For, sometimes of an afternoon when Miss Pupford has been reading the paper through her little gold eyeglass (it is necessary to read it on the spot, as the boy calls for it, with ill-conditioned punctuality, in an hour), she has become agitated, and has said to her assistant, " G !" Then Miss Pupford's assistant has gone to Miss Pupford, and Miss Pupford has pointed out, with her eye-glass, G in the paper, and then Miss Pupford's assistant has read about G, and has shown sympathy. So stimulated has the pupil-mind been in its time to curiosity on the subject of G, that once, under temporary circumstances favourable to the bold sally, one fearless pupil did actually obtain possession of the paper, and range all over it in search of G, who had been discovered therein by Miss Pupford not ten minutes before. But no G could be identified except one capital offender who had been executed in a state of great hardihood, and it was not to be supposed that Miss Pupford could ever have loved *him*. Besides,

he couldn't be always being executed. Besides, he got into the paper again, alive, within a month.

On the whole, it is suspected by the pupil-mind that G is a short chubby old gentleman, with little black sealing-wax boots up to his knees, whom a sharply observant pupil, Miss Linx, when she once went to Tunbridge Wells with Miss Pupford for the holidays, reported on her return (privately and confidentially) to have seen come capering up to Miss Pupford on the Promenade, and to have detected in the act of squeezing Miss Pupford's hand, and to have heard pronounce the words, " Cruel Euphemia, ever thine!"—or something like that. Miss Linx hazarded a guess that he might be House of Commons, or Money Market, or Court Circular, or Fashionable Movements; which would account for his getting into the paper so often. But, it was fatally objected by the pupil-mind, that none of those notabilities could possibly be spelt with a G.

There are other occasions, closely watched and perfectly comprehended by the pupil-mind, when Miss Pupford imparts with mystery to her assistant that there is special excitement in the morning paper. These occasions are, when Miss Pupford finds an old pupil coming out under the head of Births or Marriages. Affectionate tears are invariably seen in Miss Pupford's meek little eyes when this is the case; and the pupil-mind, perceiving that its order has distinguished itself —though the fact is never mentioned by Miss Pupford—becomes elevated, and feels that it likewise is reserved for greatness.

Miss Pupford's assistant with the Parisian accent has a little more bone than Miss Pupford, but is of the same trim orderly diminutive cast, and from long contemplation, admiration, and imitation of Miss Pupford, has grown like her. Being entirely, devoted to Miss Pupford, and having a pretty talent for pencil-drawing, she once made a portrait of that lady: which was so instantly identified and hailed by the pupils, that it was done on stone at five shillings. Surely the softest and milkiest stone that ever was quarried, received that likeness of Miss Pupford! The lines of her placid little nose are so undecided in it that strangers to the work of art are observed to be exceedingly perplexed as to where the nose goes to, and involuntarily feel their own noses in a disconcerted manner. Miss Pupford being represented in a state of dejection at an open window, ruminating over a bowl of gold-fish, the pupil-mind has settled that the bowl was presented by G, and that he wreathed the bowl with flowers of soul, and that Miss Pupford is depicted as waiting for him on a memorable occasion when he was behind his time.

The approach of the last Midsummer holidays had a particular interest for the pupil-mind, by reason of its knowing that Miss Pupford was bidden on the second day of those holidays, to the nuptials of a former pupil. As it was impossible to conceal the fact—so extensive were the dress-making preparations—Miss Pupford openly announced it. But, she held it due to parents to make the announcement with an air of gentle melancholy, as if marriage were (as indeed it exceptionally has been) rather a calamity. With an air of softened resignation and pity, therefore, Miss Pupford went on with her preparations; and meanwhile no pupil ever went up-stairs, or came down, without peeping in at the door of Miss Pupford's bed-room (when Miss Pupford wasn't there) and bringing back some surprising intelligence concerning the bonnet.

The extensive preparations being completed on the day before the holidays, an unanimous entreaty was preferred to Miss Pupford by the pupil-mind—finding expression through Miss Pupford's assistant—that she would deign to appear in all her splendour. Miss Pupford consenting, presented a lovely spectacle. And although the oldest pupil was barely thirteen, every one of the six became in two minutes perfect in the shape, cut, colour, price, and quality, of every article Miss Pupford wore.

Thus delightfully ushered in, the holidays began. Five of the six pupils kissed little Kitty Kimmeens twenty times over (round total, one hundred times, for she was very popular,) and so went home. Miss Kitty Kimmeens remained behind, for her relations and friends were all in India, far away. A self-helpful steady little child is Miss Kitty Kimmeens: a dimpled child too, and a loving.

So, the great marriage-day came, and Miss Pupford, quite as much fluttered as any bride could be (G! thought Miss Kitty Kimmeens), went away, splendid to behold, in the carriage that was sent for her. But not Miss Pupford only went away; for Miss Pupford's assistant went away with her, on a dutiful visit to an aged uncle—though surely the venerable gentleman couldn't live in the gallery of the church where the marriage was to be, thought Miss Kitty Kimmeens—and yet Miss Pupford's assistant had let out that she was going there. Where the cook was going, didn't appear, but she generally conveyed to Miss Kimmeens that she was bound, rather against her will, on a pilgrimage to perform some pious office that rendered new ribbons necessary to her best bonnet, and also sandals to her shoes.

"So you see," said the housemaid, when they were all gone, "there's nobody left in the house but you and me, Miss Kimmeens."

"Nobody else," said Miss Kitty Kimmeens, shaking her curls a little sadly. "Nobody!"

"And you wouldn't like your Bella to go too; would you, Miss Kimmeens?" said the housemaid. (She being Bella.)

"N—no," answered little Miss Kimmeens.

"Your poor Bella is forced to stay with you, whether she likes it or not; ain't she, Miss Kimmeens?"

"*Don't* you like it?" inquired Kitty.

"Why, you're such a darling. Miss, that it would be unkind of your Bella to make objections. Yet my brother-in-law has been took unexpected bad by this morning's post. And your poor Bella is much attached to him, letting alone her favourite sister, Miss Kimmeens."

"Is he very ill?" asked little Kitty.

"Your poor Bella has her fears so, Miss Kimmeens," returned the housemaid, with her apron at her eyes. "It was but his inside, it is true, but it might mount, and the doctor said that if it mounted he wouldn't answer." Here the housemaid was so overcome that Kitty administered the only comfort she had ready: which was a kiss.

"If it hadn't been for disappointing Cook, dear Miss Kimmeens," said the housemaid, "your Bella would have asked her to stay with you. For Cook is sweet company, Miss Kimmeens; much more so than your own poor Bella."

"But you are very nice, Bella."

"Your Bella could wish to be so, Miss Kimmeens," returned the housemaid, "but she knows full well that it do not lay in her power this day."

With which despondent conviction, the housemaid drew a heavy sigh, and shook her head, and dropped it on one side.

"If it had been anyways right to disappoint Cook," she pursued, in a contemplative and abstracted manner, "it might have been so easy done! I could have got to my brother-in-law's, and had the best part of the day there, and got back, long before our ladies come home at night, and neither the one nor the other of them need never have known it. Not that Miss Pupford would at all object, but that it might put her out, being tender-hearted. Hows'ever, your own poor Bella, Miss Kimmeens," said the housemaid, rousing herself, "is forced to stay with you, and you're a precious love, if not a liberty."

"Bella," said little Kitty, after a short silence.

"Call your own poor Bella, *your* Bella, dear," the housemaid besought her.

"My Bella, then."

"Bless your considerate heart!" said the housemaid.

"If you would not mind leaving me, I should not mind being left. I am not afraid to stay in the house alone. And you need not be uneasy on my account, for I would be very careful to do no harm."

"Oh! As to harm, you more than sweetest, if not a liberty," exclaimed the housemaid, in a rapture, "your Bella could trust you anywhere, being so steady and so answerable. The oldest head in this house (me and Cook says), but for its bright hair, is Miss Kimmeens. But no, I will not leave you; for you would think your Bella unkind."

"But if you are my Bella, you *must* go," returned the child.

"Must I?" said the housemaid, rising, on the whole with alacrity. "What must be, must be, Miss Kimmeens. Your own poor Bella acts according, though unwilling. But go or stay, your own poor Bella loves you, Miss Kimmeens."

It was certainly go, and not stay, for within five minutes Miss Kimmeens' own poor Bella—so much improved in point of spirits as to have grown almost sanguine on the subject of her brother-in-law—went her way, in apparel that seemed to have been expressly prepared for some festive occasion. Such are the changes of this fleeting world, and so short-sighted are we poor mortals!

When the house door closed with a bang and a shake, it seemed to Miss Kimmeens to be a very heavy house door, shutting her up in a wilderness of a house. But Miss Kimmeens being, as before stated, of a self reliant and methodical character, presently began to parcel out the long summer-day before her.

And first she thought she would go all over the house, to make quite sure that nobody with a great-coat on and a carving-knife in it, had got under one of the beds or into one of the cupboards. Not that she had ever before been troubled by the image of anybody armed with a great-coat and a carving-knife, but that it seemed to have been shaken into existence by the shake and the bang of the great street door, reverberating through the solitary house. So, little Miss Kimmeens looked under the five empty beds of the five departed pupils, and looked under her own bed, and looked under Miss Pupford's bed, and looked under Miss Pupford's assistant's bed. And when she had done this, and was making the tour of the cupboards, the disagreeable thought came into her young head, What a very alarming thing it would be to find somebody with a mask on, like Guy Fawkes, hiding bolt upright in a corner and pretending not to be alive! However, Miss Kimmeens having finished her inspection without making any such uncomfortable discovery, sat down in her tidy little manner to needlework, and began stitching away at a great rate.

The silence all about her soon grew very oppressive, and the more so because of the odd inconsistency that the more silent it was, the more noises there were. The noise of her own needle and thread as she stitched, was infinitely louder in her ears than the stitching of all the six pupils, and of Miss Pupford, and of Miss Pupford's assistant, all stitching away at once on a highly emulative afternoon. Then, the schoolroom clock conducted itself in a way in which it had never conducted itself before—fell lame, somehow, and yet persisted in running on as hard and as loud as it could: the consequence of which behaviour was, that it staggered among the minutes in a state of the greatest confusion, and knocked them about in all directions without appearing to get on with its regular work. Perhaps this alarmed the stairs; but be that as it might, they began to creek in a most unusual manner, and then the furniture began to crack, and then poor little Miss Kimmeens, not liking the furtive aspect of things in general, began to sing as she stitched. But, it was not her own voice that she heard—it was somebody else making believe to be Kitty, and singing excessively flat, without any heart—so, as that would never mend matters, she left off again.

By-and-by, the stitching became so palpable a failure that Miss Kitty Kimmeens folded her work neatly, and put it away in its box, and gave it up. Then the question arose about reading. But no; the book that was so delightful when there was somebody she loved for her eyes to fall on when they rose from the page, had not more heart in it than her own singing now. The book went to its shelf as the needlework had gone to its box, and, since something

must be done—thought the child, "I'll go get my room to rights."

She shared her room with her dearest little friend among the other five pupils, and why then should she now conceive a lurking dread of the little friend's bedstead? But, she did. There was a stealthy air about its innocent white curtains, and there were even dark hints of a dead girl lying under the coverlet. The great want of human company, the great need of a human face, began now to express itself in the facility with which the furniture put on strange exaggerated resemblances to human looks. A chair with a menacing frown was horribly out of temper in a corner; a most vicious chest of drawers snarled at her from between the windows. It was no relief to escape from those monsters to the looking-glass, for the reflexion said, "What! Is that you all alone there! How you stare!" And the background was all a great void stare as well.

The day dragged on, dragging Kitty with it very slowly by the hair of her head, until it was time to eat. There were good provisions in the pantry, but their right flavour and relish had evaporated with the five pupils, and Miss Pupford, and Miss Pupford's assistant, and the cook and housemaid. Where was the use of laying the cloth symmetrically for one small guest, who had gone on ever since the morning growing smaller and smaller, while the empty house had gone on swelling larger and larger? The very Grace came out wrong, for who were "we" who were going to receive and be thankful? So, Miss Kimmeens was not thankful, and found herself taking her dinner in very slovenly style—gobbling it up, in short, rather after the manner of the lower animals, not to particularise the pigs.

But, this was by no means the worst of the change wrought out in the naturally loving and cheery little creature as the solitary day wore on. She began to brood and be suspicious. She discovered that she was full of wrongs and injuries. All the people she knew, got tainted by her lonely thoughts and turned bad.

It was all very well for Papa, a widower in India, to send her home to be educated, and to pay a handsome round sum every year for her to Miss Pupford, and to write charming letters to his darling little daughter; but what did he care for her being left by herself, when he was (as no doubt he always was) enjoying himself in company from morning till night? Perhaps he only sent her here, after all, to get her out of the way. It looked like it—looked like it to-day, that is, for she had never dreamed of such a thing before.

And this old pupil who was being married. It was insupportably conceited and selfish in the old pupil to be married. She was very vain, and very glad to show off; but it was highly probable she wasn't pretty; and even if she were pretty (which Miss Kimmeens now totally denied), she had no business to be married; and, even if marriage were conceded, she had no business to ask Miss Pupford to her wedding. As to Miss Pupford, she was too old to go to any wedding. She ought to know that. She had

much better attend to her business. She had
thought she looked nice in the morning, but she
didn't look nice. She was a stupid old thing.
G was another stupid old thing. Miss Pupford's
assistant was another. They were all stupid
old things together.

More than that: it began to be obvious that
this was a plot. They had said to one another,
"Never mind Kitty; you get off, and I'll get
off; and we'll leave Kitty to look after herself.
Who cares for her?" To be sure they were right
in that question; for who did care for her, a
poor little lonely thing against whom they all
planned and plotted? Nobody, nobody! Here
Kitty sobbed.

At all other times she was the pet of the whole
house, and loved her five companions in return
with a child's tenderness and most ingenuous
attachment; but now the five companions put
on ugly colours, and appeared for the first time
under a sullen cloud. There they were, all at
their homes that day, being made much of,
being taken out, being spoilt and made disagreeable, and caring nothing for her! It was like
their artful selfishness always to tell her when
they came back, under pretence of confidence and
friendship, all those details about where they
had been, and what they had done and seen,
and how often they had said "Oh! If we had
only darling little Kitty here!" Here indeed!
I dare say! When they came back after the
holidays, they were used to being petted by
Kitty, and to saying that coming to Kitty was
like coming to another home. Very well then,
why did they go away? If they meant it, why
did they go away? Let them answer that. But
they didn't mean it, and couldn't answer that,
and they didn't tell the truth, and people who
didn't tell the truth were hateful. When they
came back next time, they should be received
in a new manner; they should be avoided and
shunned.

And there, the while she sat all alone revolving how ill she was used, and how much better
she was than the people who were not alone,
the wedding breakfast was going on; no question of it! With a nasty great bride-cake, and
with those ridiculous orange-flowers, and with
that conceited bride, and that hideous bride-
groom, and those heartless bridesmaids, and Miss
Pupford stuck up at the table! They thought
they were enjoying themselves, but it would
come home to them one day to have thought so.
They would all be dead in a few years, let them
enjoy themselves ever so much. It was a reli-
gious comfort to know that.

It was such a comfort to know it, that little
Miss Kitty Kimmeens suddenly sprang from the
chair in which she had been musing in a corner,
and cried out, "O those envious thoughts are
not mine! O this wicked creature isn't me! Help
me somebody! I go wrong, alone by my weak
self. Help me anybody!"

"— Miss Kimmeens is not a professed philo-
sopher, sir," said Mr. Traveller, presenting her at
the barred window, and smoothing her shining
hair, "but I apprehend there was some tinc-
ture of philosophy in her words, and in the

prompt action with which she followed them.
That action was, to emerge from her unnatural
solitude, and look abroad for wholesome sympathy, to bestow and to receive. Her footsteps
strayed to this gate, bringing her here by chance,
as an apposite contrast to you. The child came
out, sir. If you have the wisdom to learn from
a child (but I doubt it, for that requires more
wisdom than one in your condition would seem
to possess), you cannot do better than imitate
the child, and come out too—from that very de-
moralising hutch of yours."

VII.

PICKING UP THE TINKER.

It was now sunset. The Hermit had betaken
himself to his bed of cinders half an hour ago,
and lying on it in his blanket and skewer with
his back to the window, took not the smallest
heed of the appeal addressed to him.

All that had been said for the last two hours,
had been said to a tinkling accompaniment performed by the Tinker, who had got to work upon
some villager's pot or kettle, and was working
briskly outside. This music still continuing,
seemed to put it into Mr. Traveller's mind to
have another word or two with the Tinker. So,
holding Miss Kimmeens (with whom he was
now on the most friendly terms) by the hand,
he went out at the gate to where the Tinker was
seated at his work on the patch of grass on the
opposite side of the road, with his wallet of tools
open before him, and his little fire smoking.

"I am glad to see you employed," said Mr.
Traveller.

"I am glad to be employed," returned the
Tinker, looking up as he put the finishing touches
to his job. "But why are you glad?"

"I thought you were a lazy fellow when I
saw you this morning."

"I was only disgusted," said the Tinker.

"Do you mean with the fine weather?"

"With the fine weather?" repeated the Tinker, staring.

"You told me you were not particular as to
weather, and I thought——"

"Ha, ha! How should such as me get on, if
we was particler as to weather? We must take
it as it comes, and make the best of it. There's
something good in all weathers. If it don't happen to be good for my work to-day, it's good for
some other man's to-day, and will come round
to me to-morrow. We must all live."

"Pray shake hands!" said Mr. Traveller.

"Take care, sir," was the Tinker's caution, as
he reached up his hand in surprise; "the black
comes off."

"I am glad of it," said Mr. Traveller. "I have
been for several hours among other black that
does not come off."

"You are speaking of Tom in there?"

"Yes."

"Well now," said the Tinker, blowing the dust

off his job: which was finished. "Ain't it enough to disgust a pig, if he could give his mind to it?"

"If he could give his mind to it," returned the other, smiling, "the probability is, that he wouldn't be a pig."

"There you clench the nail," returned the Tinker. "Then what's to be said for Tom?"

"Truly, very little."

"Truly nothing you mean, sir," said the Tinker, as he put away his tools.

"A better answer, and (I freely acknowledge) my meaning. I infer that he was the cause of your disgust?"

"Why, look'ee here, sir," said the Tinker, rising to his feet, and wiping his face on the corner of his black apron energetically; "I leave you to judge!—I ask you!—Last night I has a job that needs to be done in the night, and I works all night. Well, there's nothing in that. But this morning I comes along this road here, looking for a sunny and soft spot to sleep in, and I sees this desolation and ruination. I've lived myself in desolation and ruination. I knows many a fellow-creetur that's forced to live, life long, in desolation and ruination; and I sits me down and takes pity on it, as I casts my eyes about. Then comes up the long-winded one as I told you of, from that gate, and spins himself out like a silkworm concerning the Donkey (if my Donkey at home will excuse me) as has made it all—made it of his own choice! And tells me, if you please, of his likewise choosing to go ragged, and naked, and grimy—masquerading, mountebanking, in what is the real hard lot of thousands and thousands! Why, then I say it's a unbearable and nonsensical piece of inconsistency, and I'm disgusted. I'm ashamed and disgusted!"

"I wish you would come and look at him," said Mr. Traveller, clapping the Tinker on the shoulder

"Not I, sir," he rejoined. "I ain't a going to flatter him up, by looking at him!"

"But he is asleep."

"Are you sure he is asleep?" asked the Tinker, with an unwilling air, as he shouldered his wallet.

"Sure."

"Then I'll look at him for a quarter of a minute," said the Tinker, "since you so much wish it; but not a moment longer."

They all three went back across the road; and, through the barred window, by the dying glow of the sunset coming in at the gate—which the child held open for its admission—he could be pretty clearly discerned lying on his bed.

"You see him?" asked Mr. Traveller.

"Yes," returned the Tinker, "and he's worse than I thought him."

Mr. Traveller then whispered in few words what he had done since morning; and asked the Tinker what he thought of that?

"I think," returned the Tinker, as he turned from the window, "that you've wasted a day on him."

"I think so too; though not, I hope, upon myself. Do you happen to be going anywhere near the Peal of Bells?"

"That's my direct way, sir," said the Tinker.

"I invite you to supper there. And as I learn from this young lady that she goes some three-quarters of a mile in the same direction, we will drop her off the road, and we will spare time to keep her company at her garden gate until her own Bella comes home."

So, Mr. Traveller, and the child, and the Tinker, went along very amicably in the sweet-scented evening; and the moral with which the Tinker dismissed the subject was, that he said in his trade, that metal that rotted for want of use had better be left to rot, and couldn't rot too soon, considering how much true metal rotted from over-use and hard service.

THE END.

CPSIA information can be obtained
at www.ICGtesting.com
Printed in the USA
BVOW08s1425051217

502032BV00013B/157/P

9 781167 166679